# 3rd NLP4IF Workshop on NLP for Internet Freedom: Censorship, Disinformation, and Propaganda (NLP4IF'2020)



Barcelona, Spain
12 December 2020

ISBN: 978-1-7138-2835-8

**Printed from e-media with permission by:**

Curran Associates, Inc.
57 Morehouse Lane
Red Hook, NY 12571

**Some format issues inherent in the e-media version may also appear in this print version.**



Printed with permission by Curran Associates, Inc. (2021)

For permission requests, please contact the Association for Computational Linguistics at the address below.

Association for Computational Linguistics
209 N. Eighth Street
Stroudsburg, Pennsylvania 18360

Phone: 1-570-476-8006
Fax: 1-570-476-0860

acl@aclweb.org

**Additional copies of this publication are available from:**

Curran Associates, Inc.
57 Morehouse Lane
Red Hook, NY 12571 USA
Phone: 845-758-0400
Fax: 845-758-2633
Email: curran@proceedings.com
Web: www.proceedings.com

COLING 2020

# Proceedings of the 3rd NLP4IF Workshop on NLP for Internet Freedom: Censorship, Disinformation, and Propaganda

**Co-located with the 28th International Conference on Computational Linguistics COLING'2020**

**NLP4IF'2020**

December 12, 2020
Barcelona, Spain (Online)

# Preface

We are living in unprecedented times. Humanity is working together to fight the pandemic. The COVID-19 pandemic has altered our way of life and how we go about our daily routines. For many, kitchen and dining room tables have become the new office, classroom, or social meeting place. Virtual is the new reality, and while it allows many of us to continue to work, learn and socialize safely, it comes with its own unique set of challenges and dangers. As we transition to using more online platforms, scammers, hackers and other cybercriminals are finding new ways to target people. With social distancing as the new norm, socialization has turned even more digital than ever before. Unfortunately, cyber bullying is rampant and has been linked to a variety of negative effects, including anxiety, depression, and substance abuse. In addition, according to Freedom House[1], disinformation campaigns have been on the rise since March 2020. Cooordinated and covert attempts by China-linked actors to manipulate information, particularly regarding COVID-19, have been detected in many countries, including the United States, Argentina, Serbia, Italy, and Taiwan, with the relevant content often delivered in local languages. Our workshop tries to address these challenges.

Vijjali et al., for example, develop a two stage automated pipiline for COVID-19 fake news detection: the first model retrieves the most relevant facts concerning user claims about specific COVID-19-related claims; the second model verifies the level of truth in the claim by computing the textual entailment between the claim and the true facts retrieved from a manually curated COVID-19 dataset. The authors demonstrate the effectiveness of pre-trained Transformer-based language models in retrieving and classifying fake news and suggest that the model performance can be further boosted by adding domain-specific knowledge.

Shin et al. describe the communication patterns on the coronvirus pandemic from three Asian countries using a time-topic cohesive model, which can detect contextualized events based on topical and temporal information via contrastive learning. It then can be applied to multiple languages, enabling a comparison of risk communication across cultures. They present a case study and discuss future implications of the proposed model.

Information warfare has recently shifted its focus to social media, but traditional media continue to play an important role. In their work with civial society organizations and journalists around the world, Niven & Kau have identified the usefulness of NLP tools to detect and to track media that are aligned with the Chinese Communist Party (CPP). Niven & Kau operationalize alignment in terms of sociological definitions of media bias. They take as a case study the alignment of four Taiwanese media outlets to the CPP state media. They present the results of an initial investigation using the frequency of words in psychologically meaningful categories. Their findings suggest that the chosen word categories correlate with framing choices.

Prakash & Madabushi propose a novel architecture for the task of stance detection, which integrates count-based features into pre-trained models such as BERT and RoBERTa, with specific regard to the identification of disinformation and propaganda on social media, where handcrafted and count-based features can be particularly helpful.

Lily et al. focus on the task of satire detection, noticing that satire is often misinterpreted by readers as legitimate news. They propose a multi-modal approach based on the state-of-the-art visiolinguistic model ViLBERT. They create a new dataset consisting of images and headlines of regular and satirical news, fine-tune ViLBERT on the dataset and train a convolutional neural network that uses an image forensics technique. Evaluation on the dataset shows that their proposed multi-modal approach outperforms image-only, text-only, and simple fusion baselines.

[1] http://freedomhouse.org/

We are also thrilled to be able to bring two invited speakers: Stephan Lewandowsky from the University of Bristol with a talk on social media coverage and human decision making and Aylin Caliskan from George Washington University with a talk on the impact of machine intelligence on society, especially threats to fairness, privacy, and democracy.

We further feature a panel including Roya Ensafi and Veronica Perez-Rosas from the University of Michigan, Andreas Vlachos from the University of Cambridge, and Stephan Lewandowsky from the University of Bristol.

Last but not least, we would like to thank the program committee for their help with reviewing the papers, and with advertising the workshop.

The NLP4IF 2020 Organizers:

Giovanni Da San Martino, Qatar Computing Research Institute, Chris Brew, Giovanni Luca Ciampaglia, Anna Feldman, Chris Leberknight, Preslav Nakov

`http://www.netcopia.net/nlp4if/`

**Organizers:**

Giovanni Da San Martino, Qatar Computing Research Institute, HBKU
Chris Brew, LivePerson
Giovanni Luca Ciampaglia, University of South Florida
Anna Feldman, Montclair State University
Chris Leberknight, Montclair State University
Preslav Nakov, Qatar Computing Research Institute, HBKU

**Program Committee:**

Tariq Alhindi, Columbia University
Alberto Barrón-Cedeño, Università di Bologna
Jedidiah Crandall, Arizona State University
Anjalie Field, Carnegie Mellon University
Yiqing Hua, Cornell Tech
Jeffrey Knockel, The University of New Mexico
Henrique Lopes Cardoso, University of Porto
Hannah Rashkin. University of Washington

**Invited Speakers:**

Aylin Caliskan, George Washington University
Stephan Lewandowsky, University of Bristol

**Panelists:**

Roya Ensafi, University of Michigan
Stephan Lewandowsky, University of Bristol
Veronica Perez-Rosas, University of Michigan
Joshua Tucker, New York University
Andreas Vlachos, University of Cambridge

## Invited Talk: Implications of Biased AI on Democracy, Equity, and Justice

Aylin Caliskan
George Washington University

**Abstract:** Billions of people on the internet are exposed to the outputs of downstream natural language processing (NLP) applications on a daily basis. Many of these NLP applications use word embeddings as general purpose language representations. In this talk, Aylin Caliskan will introduce the Word Embedding Association Test (WEAT) to demonstrate that word embeddings trained on language corpora embed the biases and associations documented by the Implicit Association Test in social psychology. In particular, WEAT measures how statistical regularities of language capture biases and stereotypes, such as racism, sexism, and attitudes toward social groups. Word embeddings are trained on text collected from the internet, that includes society's organic natural language data in addition to text from information influence operations. The adaptation of WEAT to the information influence domain automatically characterizes overall attitudes and biases associated with emerging information influence operations. Accurate analysis of these emerging topics usually requires laborious, manual analysis by experts to annotate a large set of data points to identify biases in new topics. We validate our practical and non-parametric method using known information operation-related tweets from Twitter's Transparency Report. We perform a case study on the COVID-19 pandemic to evaluate our method's performance on non-labeled Twitter data, demonstrating its usability in emerging domains.

**Bio:** Aylin Caliskan is an Assistant Professor of Computer Science at George Washington University. Her research interests lie in AI ethics, bias in AI, machine learning, and the implications of machine intelligence on fairness and privacy. She investigates the reasoning behind biased AI representations and decisions by developing explainability methods that uncover and quantify biases of machines. Building these transparency enhancing algorithms involves the heavy use of machine learning, natural language processing, and computer vision in novel ways to interpret AI and gain insights about bias in machines as well as society. In her recent publication in Science, she demonstrated how semantics derived from language corpora contain human-like biases. Prior to that, she developed novel privacy attacks to de-anonymize programmers using code stylometry. Her presentations on both de-anonymization and bias in machine learning are the recipients of best talk awards. Her work on semi-automated anonymization of writing style furthermore received the Privacy Enhancing Technologies Symposium Best Paper Award. Aylin holds a PhD in Computer Science from Drexel University and a Master of Science in Robotics from the University of Pennsylvania. Before joining the faculty at George Washington University, she was a Postdoctoral Researcher and a Fellow at Princeton University's Center for Information Technology Policy.

# Invited Talk: Diversionary Agenda Setting and Micro-Targeted Persuasion

Stephan Lewandowsky
University of Bristol

**Abstract:** We are said to live in a "post-truth" era in which "fake news" has replaced real information, denial has compromised science, and the ontology of knowledge and truth has taken on a relativist element. I argue that to defend evidence-based reasoning and knowledge against those attacks, we must understand the strategies by which the post-truth world is driven forward. I depart from the premise that the post-truth era did not arise spontaneously but is the result of a highly effective political movement that deploys a large number of rhetorical strategies. I focus on two strategies: Diversionary agenda-setting by social media and the use of "micro-targeting" of political messages online. I present evidence for the existence of each strategy and its impact, and how it might be countered.

**Bio:** Professor Stephan Lewandowsky is a cognitive scientist at the University of Bristol. He was an Australian Professorial Fellow from 2007 to 2012, and was awarded a Discovery Outstanding Researcher Award from the Australian Research Council in 2011. His research examines people's memory, decision making, and knowledge structures, with a particular emphasis on how people update information in memory. His most recent research interests examine the potential conflict between human cognition and the physics of the global climate, which has led him into research in climate science and climate modeling. He has published more than 200 scholarly articles, chapters, and books, including numerous papers on how people respond to corrections of misinformation and what variables determine people's acceptance of scientific findings. Professor Lewandowsky is an award-winning teacher and was Associate Editor of the Journal of Experimental Psychology: Learning, Memory, and Cognition from 2006-2008. He has also contributed around 50 opinion pieces to the global media on issues related to climate change "skepticism" and the coverage of science in the media. He is currently serving as Digital Content Editor for the Psychonomic Society and blogs routinely on cognitive research.

## Panelists

**Roya Ensafi** is an assistant professor in computer science and engineering at the University of Michigan, where her research focuses on computer networking, security, and privacy. Her notable projects with real-world impact include founding Censored Planet, a global censorship observatory, and researching the Kazakhstan HTTPS MitM interception, the Great Cannon of China, and large-scale study of server-side geoblocking. She has received the NSF CISE Research Initiation Initiative award, the Google Faculty Research Award, and Consumer Report Digital Lab fellowship. Roya's work has appeared in the popular press publications such as the NY Times, Wired, Business Insider, and ArsTechnica.

**Stephan Lewandowsky** (see above for his biography)

**Veronica Perez-Rosas** is an assistant research scientist at the University of Michigan. Her research interests include machine learning, natural language processing, computational linguistics, affect recognition, and multimodal analysis of human behavior. Her research focuses on developing computational methods to analyze, recognize, and predict human affective responses during social interactions. She has authored papers in leading conferences and journals in Natural Language Processing and Computational Linguistics, and she served as a program committee member for multiple international journals and conferences in the same fields.

**Joshua Tucker** is Professor of Politics, affiliated Professor of Russian and Slavic Studies, and affiliated Professor of Data Science at New York University. He is the Director of NYU's Jordan Center for Advanced Study of Russia, a co-Director of the NYU Center for Social Media and Politics, and a co-author/editor of the award-winning politics and policy blog The Monkey Cage at The Washington Post. He serves on the advisory board of the American National Election Study, the Comparative Study of Electoral Systems, and numerous academic journals, and was the co-founder and co-editor of the Journal of Experimental Political Science. His original research was on mass political behavior in post-communist countries, including voting and elections, partisanship, public opinion formation, and protest participation. More recently, he has been at the forefront of the newly emerging field of study of the relationship between social media and politics. His research in this area has included studies on the effects of network diversity on tolerance, partisan echo chambers, online hate speech, the effects of exposure to social media on political knowledge, online networks and protest, disinformation and fake news, how authoritarian regimes respond to online opposition, and Russian bots and trolls, and he is currently the co-Chair of the independent academic advisory board of the 2020 Facebook Election Research Study. An internationally recognized scholar, he has served as a keynote speaker for conferences in Sweden, Denmark, Italy, Brazil, the Netherlands, Russia, and the United States, and has given more than 100 invited research presentations at top domestic and international universities and research centers over the past decade. His research has appeared in over two-dozen scholarly journals and has been supported by a wide range of philanthropic foundations, as well as multiple grants from the National Science Foundation. His most recent books are the co-authored Communism's Shadow: Historical Legacies and Contemporary Political Attitudes (Princeton University Press, 2017), and the co-edited Social Media and Democracy: The State of the Field (Cambridge University Press, 2020).

**Andreas Vlachos** is a senior lecturer at the Natural Language and Information Processing group at the Department of Computer Science and Technology at the University of Cambridge. Current projects include dialogue modelling, automated fact checking and imitation learning. He has also worked on semantic parsing, natural language generation and summarization, language modelling, information extraction, active learning, clustering, and biomedical text mining. His research is supported by ERC, EPSRC, ESRC, Facebook, Amazon, Google and Huawei.

# Table of Contents

# Conference Program

*Two Stage Transformer Model for COVID-19 Fake News Detection and Fact Checking*
Rutvik Vijjali, Prathyush Potluri, Siddharth Kumar and Sundeep Teki

*Measuring Alignment to Authoritarian State Media as Framing Bias*
Timothy Niven and Hung-Yu Kao

*Incorporating Count-Based Features into Pre-Trained Models for Improved Stance Detection*
Anushka Prakash and Harish Tayyar Madabushi

*A Multi-Modal Method for Satire Detection using Textual and Visual Cues*
Lily Li, Or Levi, Pedram Hosseini and David Broniatowski

*A Risk Communication Event Detection Model via Contrastive Learning*
Mingi Shin, Sungwon Han, Sungkyu Park and Meeyoung Cha

# Two Stage Transformer Model for COVID-19 Fake News Detection and Fact Checking

**Rutvik Vijjali*** rutvikvijjali30@gmail.com

**Prathyush Potluri*** potluri.prathyush@gmail.com

**Siddharth Kumar*** kumar.sidiyer@gmail.com

**Sundeep Teki** sundeep.teki@gmail.com

## Abstract

The rapid advancement of technology in online communication via social media platforms has led to a prolific rise in the spread of misinformation and fake news. Fake news is especially rampant in the current COVID-19 pandemic, leading to people believing in false and potentially harmful claims and stories. Detecting fake news quickly can alleviate the spread of panic, chaos and potential health hazards. We developed a two stage automated pipeline for COVID-19 fake news detection using state of the art machine learning models for natural language processing. The first model leverages a novel fact checking algorithm that retrieves the most relevant facts concerning user claims about particular COVID-19 claims. The second model verifies the level of "truth" in the claim by computing the textual entailment between the claim and the true facts retrieved from a manually curated COVID-19 dataset. The dataset is based on a publicly available knowledge source consisting of more than 5000 COVID-19 false claims and verified explanations, a subset of which was internally annotated and cross-validated to train and evaluate our models. We evaluate a series of models based on classical text-based features to more contextual Transformer based models and observe that a model pipeline based on BERT and ALBERT for the two stages respectively yields the best results.

## 1 Introduction

Electronic means of communication have helped to eliminate time and distance barriers to sharing and broadcasting information. However, despite all its advantages, faster means of communication has also resulted in extensive spread of misinformation. The world is currently going through the deadly COVID-19 pandemic and fake news regarding the disease, its cures, its prevention and causes have been broadcast widely to millions of people. The spread of fake news and misinformation during such precarious times can have grave consequences leading to widespread panic and amplification of the threat of the pandemic itself. It is therefore of paramount importance to limit the spread of fake news and ensure that accurate knowledge is disseminated to the public.

In this work, we propose a robust, dynamic fake news detection system, that can not only estimate the "correctness" of a claim but also provides users with pertinent information regarding the said claim. This is achieved using a knowledge base of verified information that can be constantly updated. Previous work on fake news detection has primarily focused on evaluating the relationship measured via a textual entailment task between a header and the body of the article. However, such a method is insufficient for identifying specific fake news claims without any knowledge of the facts relevant to the claim. This warrants the use of a new dataset specific to the COVID-19 pandemic.

Developing a solution for such a task involves generating a database of factual explanations, which becomes our knowledge base, that serves as ground truth for any given claim. We compute the entailment between any given claim and explanation to verify if the claim is true or not. Querying for claim, explanation pairs for each explanation in our knowledge base is computationally expensive and slow, so

* These authors contributed equally.





*Proceedings of the 3rd NLP4IF Workshop on NLP for Internet Freedom*, pages 1–10
Barcelona, Spain (Online), December 12, 2020

we propose generating a set of candidate explanations which are contextually similar to the claim. We achieve this by using a model trained with relevant and irrelevant claim explanation pairs, and using a similarity metric between the two to match them. Therefore, in the pipeline, firstly, for a given claim, a set of candidate explanations from the knowledge base have to be fetched in real-time. Then, the claim validated for truth using relevant candidate explanations. In this work, we have explored the use of Transformer (Vaswani et al., 2017) based models to both fetch relevant explanations as well as measure the entailment between a given claim and a factual explanation.

We then evaluate our model on the basis of count of relevant explanation results fetched as well as the accuracy in verifying a given claim. We demonstrate the effectiveness of pre-trained multi-attention models in terms of overall accuracy when compared with other natural language processing (NLP) baselines while maintaining near real-time performance.

## 2 Related Work

The paper (Riedel et al., 2017) uses traditional approaches with a simple classifier model that makes use of Term Frequency(TF), Term Frequency and Inverse Document Frequency(TF-IDF), and cosine similarity between vectors as features to classify fake news. They have provided a baseline for fake news stance detection on Fake News Challenge (FNC-1) dataset[1]. We have implemented their approach on our dataset and results can be seen in Table 3.

In (Nie et al., 2019), the authors present a connected system consisting of three homogeneous neural semantic matching models that perform document retrieval, sentence selection, and claim verification on the FEVER Dataset (Thorne et al., 2018) jointly for fact extraction and verification. Their Neural Semantic Matching Network (NSMN) is a modification of the Enhanced Sequential Inference Model (ESIM) (Chen et al., 2017), where they add skip connections from input to matching layer and change output layer to only max-pool plus one affine layer with ReLU activation. They use three stage pipeline in which given a claim, they first retrieve candidate documents from the corpus, followed by retrieving candidate sentences from the selected candidate documents and finally, the last stage classifies the sentence in to one of three classes. They used Bidirectional LSTM (BiLSTM) to encode the claim and sentences using GloVe (Pennington et al., 2014) and ELMO (Peters et al., 2018) embeddings. However, these tasks are concerned with static or slowly evolving domains, on topics that do not require domain expertise to annotate.

Despite the partial success of the above methods, there were still certain shortcomings in terms of the accuracy of the results. Bidirectional encoder representations from Transformers (BERT) (Devlin et al., 2018) is a pre-trained language model trained on a large corpus comprising the Wikipedia and Toronto Book Corpus, and is shown to perform well on several natural language tasks like GLUE (Wang et al., 2018). Transformer based pretrained models achieved state of the art results in several NLP subtasks, their ease of fine-tuning makes them adaptable to newer tasks. In (Jwa et al., 2019), the authors propose a model based on the BERT architecture to detect fake news by analyzing the contextual relationship between the headline and the body text of news. They demonstrate that using Transformer based models like BERT and fine-tuning them for the task of fake news detection gives better results than other models like stackLSTM (Hanselowski et al., 2018; Hermans and Schrauwen, 2013) and featMLP (Davis and Proctor, 2017). They further enhanced their model performance by pre-training with domain specific news and articles, and countered the class imbalance for the final classification task by the use of a weighted cross entropy loss function. However, this approach can not be adapted for our task of fetching relevant explanations for each claim.

(Naudé, 2020) and (Bullock et al., 2020) extensively studied the use of machine learning strategies to address various issues regarding COVID-19. The latter also describes fake news and misinformation as a major issue in the ongoing pandemic and further highlights the problem as solving an infodemic. In (Gallotti et al., 2020), the authors develop an Infodemic Risk Index (IRI) after analyzing Twitter posts

[1] http://www.fakenewschallenge.org/

**Example 1**

**False claim**: *The title of an article suggests the low - cost steroid dexamethasone will heal anybody with COVID-19 .*
**True claim**: *Steroid dexamethasone is not proven cure covid-19, it has shown to help critically ill patients only.*
**Explanation**: *Steroid dexamethasone was found to be effective only on critically - ill COVID-19 patients that require ventilators and supplemental oxygen . There was no observed benefit on patients who did not require respiratory support .*

**Example 2**

**False claim**: *Salty and sour foods cause the " body of the COVID-19 virus " to explode and dissolve .*
**True claim**: *Salty and sour foods do not help prevent or cure COVID-19.*
**Explanation**: *Consuming fruit juices or gargling with warm water and salt does not protect or kill COVID-19 , the World Health Organization Philippines told VERA Files .*

Figure 1: Cross validated data examples

across various languages and calculate the rate at which a particular user from a locality comes across unreliable posts from different classes of users like verified humans, unverified humans, verified bots, and unverified bots. In (Mejova et al., 2018), the authors examine Facebook advertisements across 64 countries and find that around 5% of advertisements contained possible errors or misinformation. But none of these mentioned works tackle the problem of misinformation by reasoning out the given fake claim with an explanation.

## 3 Dataset

Using an existing misinformation dataset will not serve as a reliable knowledge base for training and evaluating the models due to the recent and uncommon nature i.e., the vocabulary used to describe the disease and the terms associated with the COVID-19 pandemic. It is important to generate real and timely datasets to ensure accurate and consistent evaluation of the methods. To overcome this drawback, we manually curated a dataset specific to COVID-19. Our proposed dataset consists of 5500 claim and explanation pairs. We describe the collection and annotation process in Section 3.1.

### 3.1 Covid-19 Claims Dataset

There are multiple sources on the web that are regularly identifying and debunking fake news on COVID-19. We scraped data from "Poynter"[2] , a fact checking website which collects fake news and debunks or fact-checks them with supporting articles from more than 70 countries, covering more than 40 languages. The Poynter website has a database exclusively for COVID-19 with over 7000 fact checks. Each fact check contains the corresponding claim that is being checked, the rating indicating the type of the claim, for example - 'False', 'Mostly False' or 'Misleading', the name of the fact checker, the explanation given for the current claim, the location of origin of the claim and the date when the fact check was done. This data can be used to update our "explanation" look-ups in a timely fashion so our database is constantly evolving as we learn more about the virus and the facts change.

For each fact check, we collect only the "claim" and the corresponding "explanation" from this database which were rated as 'False' or 'Misleading'. In this way, we collected about 5500 false-claim and explanation pairs. We further manually rephrase these false claims to generate true claims, as the ones that align with the explanation so as to create an equal proportion of true-claim and explanation pairs. We have taken claim-explanation pairs from the time period between January 1,2020 to May

[2]https://www.poynter.org/ifcn-covid-19-misinformation/

| Dataset | Number of sentence pairs |
|---|---|
| False claim - Explanation pairs | 5500 |
| Cross validated False claim - True claim - Explanation pairs for train data | 1000 |
| Cross validated False claim - True claim - Explanation pairs for test data | 200 |

Table 1: Dataset Information

15,2020 for our training data and from May 18,2020 to July 1,2020 for our test data. In this way, we evaluate the generalization of the model on completely new and unseen data. Our collected data follows the structure:

*[false claim, explanation]*

The subset of the data that we annotated and cross validated follows the structure:

*[false claim, true claim, explanation]*

Figure 1 shows some examples of the cross validated data.

### 3.2 Dataset Statistics

The current proposed Covid-19 dataset contains cross-validated claim-explanation sentence pairs. Statistics about the distribution of labels are provided in Table 1. This is a dynamic dataset and we are continually collecting and curating additional claim-explanation pairs. We plan to open source this dataset to facilitate more research in this domain.

## 4 Methodology

The architecture consists of a two stage model, we will refer to the first model as "Model A" and the second model as "Model B". The objective of Model A is to fetch the candidate "true facts" or explanations for a given claim, which are then evaluated for entailment using the Model B. Next, we describe the training procedure as well as intended run time behaviour for both Model A and Model B.

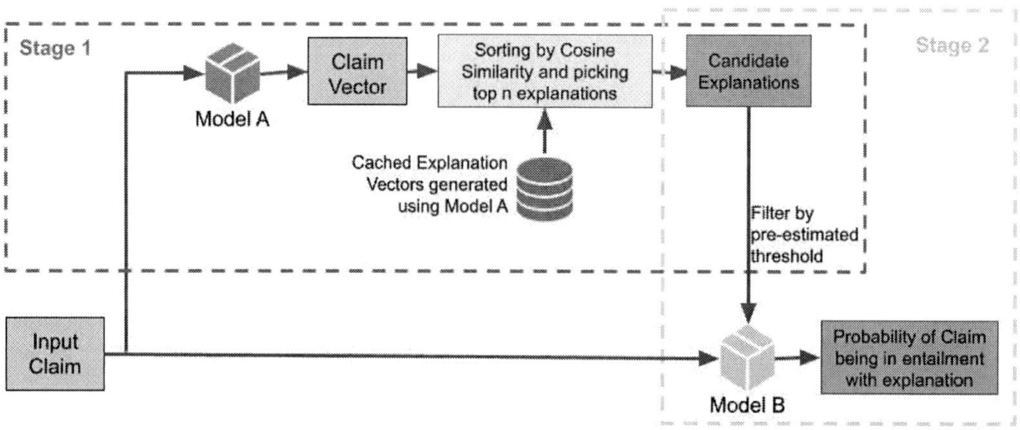


Figure 2: Block diagram of our two stage model pipeline

### 4.1 Model A

First, to fetch relevant explanations, we train our Transformer model on a binary sentence entailment task, where the claims and explanations are the two sentences fed in as input separated by a [SEP] tag. We generate negative claim-explanation pairs through random sampling to ensure that equal proportions of positive and negative pairs are present. Training multi-attention network with our COVID-19 specific data enables the model to capture long-range correlations between the vector representations of claims and explanations of similar contexts. We train our models with a base encoder and a sequence classification head on top for binary classification of the labels. The model is trained to optimise the cross entropy loss.

Through our experiments, we find that, on this trained model, if we generate embeddings for a single sentence (either claim or explanation individually) and compare matching [claim, explanation] embeddings using the cosine similarity metric, there is a distinction in the distribution of similarity scores between related and unrelated [claim,explanation] pairs. Therefore, for faster near real-time performance, we cache the embeddings for all our explanations (knowledge base) beforehand, and compute the cosine similarity between the claim and the cached embeddings of the explanations. The vector of the [CLS](the start of sentence) token of the final layer works as a strong representation of the entire sentence, although we found that taking element-wise mean over all the token vectors leads to better performance. We fetch the top explanations for any given claim exceeding a certain threshold of sentence similarity as there could be several explanations relevant for a given claim. This threshold is determined on the basis of the summary statistics of the cosine similarity metric between the claim and relevant explanations in the validation set, as described in Section 5.3. These retrieved explanations serve as candidates for verifying the accuracy of the claim through Model B.

### 4.2 Model B

The second part of the pipeline is to identify the veracity of a given claim. Model A fetches the candidate explanations while Model B is used to verify whether the given claim aligns with our set of candidate explanations or not. We can therefore treat this task as a textual entailment problem (Dagan et al., 2013; Adler et al., 2012). To train the Model B, we use a smaller subset of "false claim" and "explanation" pairs from our original dataset, and cross validate each sample with "true claim" or in other words, claims that align with the factual explanation. However, this small annotated data is not sufficient to train the model effectively. Therefore, the parameters of the Model A, which was trained on a much larger dataset were used as initial parameters for Model B, and fine-tuned further using our cross validated dataset.

We trained Model B in a similar fashion as Model A i.e. as a sequence classification problem with cross entropy loss. Once we have the candidate explanations for a given claim, we use Model B to estimate the probabilities of alignment of claim with each of the candidate explanations. We used the statistic of mean probability score and standard deviation of aligning and non-aligning claim and explanation pairs in the validation set to determine the thresholds for Model B classification. We trained and evaluated both Model A and Model B using several approaches based on classical NLP methods as well as more sophisticated pre-trained Transformer models. The flow of the Model A + Model B pipeline is shown in Figure 2.

## 5 Experiments

### 5.1 Baseline Models

For baselining our model on classical NLP approaches, we use two simple bag-of-words (BOW) representations for the text inputs: term frequency (TF) and term frequency-inverse document frequency (TF-IDF). We followed the architecture proposed by (Riedel et al., 2017). The representations and features extracted from the claim and explanation pairs consist of the following: • The TF vector of the claim; • The TF vector of the explanation; • The cosine similarity between the 2-normalised TF-IDF vectors of the claim and explanation.

For the TF vectors, we extract a vocabulary of the 5,000 most frequent words in the training set and exclude stop words (the NLTK (Bird et al., 2009) stop words for the English language). For the TF-IDF vectors, we use the same vocabulary and set of stop words. The TF vectors and the TF-IDF cosine similarity values are concatenated to form a feature vector with total dimension of 10,001 and is fed to the classifier.

The classifier takes an input of 10,001 dimensional vector followed by a feed-forward network with 50, 20 and 2 dimensional dense layers respectively with each hidden layer having tanh activation and the last layer is a softmax layer. We trained in mini-batches over the entire training set using the Adam

| Model | Model A Val Accuracy | Model B Val Accuracy |
|---|---|---|
| TF-IDF | 0.832 | 0.799 |
| GloVe | 0.781 | 0.777 |
| MobileBERT | 0.921 | 0.877 |
| ALBERT | 0.927 | **0.956** |
| BERT | **0.944** | 0.927 |

Table 2: Model Performance on Validation Set

optimiser (Kingma and Ba, 2014) with a learning rate of 0.001.
The second approach involves use of word vectors for which we used 300-dimensional GloVe (Pennington et al., 2014) embeddings, pretrained on 2014-Wikipedia and Gigaword, and averaged over token embeddings to compute sentence vectors. So, for a given claim and explanation pair, we have a 300-dimension vector for claim as well as the explanation, both of which are concatenated to form a 600-dimensional vector that serves as input to our dense layer classifier. This model is a simple feed-forward neural network with 4 hidden layers having 200, 100, 50 and 2 hidden units respectively with the first three layers having ReLU activation while the last layer is a softmax layer. We trained in mini-batches of 32 over the entire training set with back-propagation using the Adam optimizer with a learning rate of 0.001.

### 5.2 Transformer Models

We trained and evaluated three Transformer based pre-trained models for both Model A and Model B using the training strategy described in Section 4. As our focus was to ensure that the proposed pipeline can be deployed effectively in a near real-time scenario, we restricted our experiments to models that could efficiently be deployed using inexpensive compute. We chose the following three models - BERT(base), ALBERT (Lan et al., 2019) and MobileBERT (Sun et al., 2020). The authors of MobileBERT demonstrated that using a teacher-student learning technique for progressive knowledge transfer from the BERT to MobileBERT model helps them achieve a task-agnostic model similar to BERT and can be deployed easily on resource limited devices due to faster inference speeds and lower memory consumption. The ALBERT model was proposed to increase the training and inference speed of BERT besides lowering the memory consumption. The authors demonstrate that the use of their parametric reduction techniques and a custom self supervised loss helps it to achieve results similar to BERT while having fewer parameters.
Model A was trained on 5000 claim-explanation pairs on the sequence classification task to optimize the softmax cross entropy loss using a learning rate of 3e-5. This trained model was then validated on a test set comprising of 1000 unseen claim-explanation pairs. The training data structure here looks like:

*[claim, relevant explanation, 1]*

*[claim, irrelevant explanation, 0]*

Model B was trained on a smaller subset of 800 cross validated [claim,explanation,label] data, on the same sequence classification task, where the label was assigned based on whether the claim aligned with the explanation - 1 or not - 0. This was validated on 200 unseen data-points. The loss function used was softmax cross-entropy with a uniform learning rate of 1e-5. The training data structure here looks like:

*[true claim, relevant explanation, 1]*

*[false claim, relevant explanation, 0]*

### 5.3 Evaluation Metrics

For evaluating the performance of the overall pipeline model, we first evaluate the performance of Model A in its ability to retrieve relevant explanation. For this we use Mean Reciprocal Rank(MRR) (Craswell, 2009) and Mean Recall @10 (Malheiros et al., 2012), that is the proportion of claims for which the relevant explanation was present in the top 10 most contextual explanation by cosine similarity and their mean inverse rank. Equation 1 shows the MRR formula for our evaluation.

$$MRR = \frac{1}{C}\sum_{i=1}^{C}\frac{1}{rank_i} \tag{1}$$

where $rank_i$ is the position of the explanation that is relevant to a particular claim according to test data and $C$ is the total number of claims.
Equation 2 shows the Recall@10 formula for our evaluation.

$$Recall@10 = \frac{1}{C}\sum_{i=1}^{C} f(\text{top-10 explanations}) \tag{2}$$

$$where$$

$$f(\text{x}) = \begin{cases} 1 & \text{if } true\_exp \in \text{x} \\ 0 & \text{otherwise} \end{cases}$$

Here, $true\_exp$ is the actual relevant explanation for a particular claim according to test data and $C$ is the total number of claims.
Once, Model A has retrieved relevant explanations, we evaluate the performance of Model B on computing the veracity of the claim. Here, we only used explanations that exceed an empirically defined threshold in cosine similarity between the claim and the explanation. Through our experiments, we found that a threshold of *mean - standard deviation of cosine similarity* over the validation data worked well for picking relevant explanations. For evaluating the accuracy, we take a mean of the output probabilities for each $claim, explanation_i$, defined by the Equation 3.

$$p_{truth} = \frac{1}{n}\sum_{i} modelB(claim, exp_i) \tag{3}$$

$$where$$
$$exp \in exp_A \mid \cos(c\_vec_A, exp\_vec_A) > t$$

Here, $exp_A$ are the top-10 explanations returned by Model A. $c\_vec_A$ and $exp\_vec_A$ are the vector representations generated by running claim and explanations individually through Model A and $t$ refers to the threshold.

### 5.4 Results and Discussion

The performance of several Transformer based models as well as classical NLP models were compared using the evaluation metrics described in Section 5.3. The results of the experiments on the test set are summarised in Table 3.

| Model | MRR | Recall@10 | Accuracy |
|---|---|---|---|
| TF-IDF | 0.477 | 0.635 | 0.525 |
| GloVe | 0.182 | 0.410 | 0.579 |
| MobileBERT | 0.561 | 0.735 | 0.710 |
| BERT | 0.632 | 0.795 | 0.810 |
| ALBERT | 0.582 | 0.675 | 0.825 |
| **BERT+ALBERT** | 0.632 | 0.795 | 0.855 |

Table 3: Model Performance on test set

The results in Table 3 clearly illustrate that Transformer based models are significantly better than classical NLP models. An interesting observation was that some models are better at retrieval of relevant

| Model | Latency per claim (in seconds) | Memory (in MB) |
|---|---|---|
| TF-IDF | 0.108 | 16 |
| GloVe | 0.003 | 990 |
| MobileBERT | 0.607 | 1200 |
| ALBERT | 2.376 | 942 |
| BERT | 3.106 | 1910 |
| BERT + ALBERT | 2.471 | 1398 |

Table 4: Model Compute performance and Memory usage

explanations while others have a better classification performance. We find that a combination of the best performing Model A (BERT) and best performing Model B (ALBERT) yielded the highest MRR, Recall@10 and Accuracy on the test set for fact checking. We however do acknowledge that our models could still make errors of two kinds: firstly, Model A might not fetch a relevant explanation which automatically means that the prediction provided by Model B is irrelevant, and secondly, Model A might have fetched the correct explanation(s) but Model B classifies it incorrectly. We show some of the errors our models made in Table 5.

Table 4 shows the memory usage and latencies of the implemented models. The memory consumption and latency per claim in the classical NLP models was observed to be quite low in comparison to the Transformer based models. This is expected due to the lower parameter size of the TF-IDF and GloVe models. Among the Transformer based models, MobileBERT had the least latency per claim as expected and explained in Section 5.2 while ALBERT consumed the least memory. The best performing BERT+ALBERT model utilized a memory of 1398MB and fetched relevant explanations of each claim in 2.471 seconds. The model latencies and memory usage were evaluated on an *Intel Xeon - 2.3GHz Single core - 2 thread* CPU.

| |
|---|
| **Claim**: *Cannabis could help prevent coronavirus infection .*<br>**True Explanation**: *The study claiming that marijuana can cure coronavirus did not pass the peer review , it was conducted on artificial human tissues and not on real organisms . It is a classic preliminary research that may even fail . The authors themselves speak of the need for further studies and research .*<br>**Top Fetched Explanation**: *The vaccine can provide stable immunity , while the presence of antibodies does not prevent reinfection .*<br>**Remark**: *Model A fetched irrelevant explanation for this claim* |
| **Claim**: *The vaccine is not the final solution against the novel coronavirus but antibodies are .*<br>**Explanation**: *The vaccine can provide stable immunity , while the presence of antibodies does not prevent reinfection .*<br>**Probability score**: *0.340*<br>**Remark**: *Model B misclassified this claim-explanation pair as True* |
| **Claim**: *WHO recommends wearing masks in public spaces to slow down the spread of coronavirus*<br>**Explanation**: *The WHO changed its position about masks by now recommending community masks in areas with many infections . And it says that masks have to be used properly and alone can't protect you from COVID-19 .*<br>**Probability score**: *0.686*<br>**Remark**: *Model B misclassified this claim-explanation pair as False* |

Table 5: BERT+ALBERT Model Faulty predictions

## 6 Conclusions and Future work

In this work, we have demonstrated the use and effectiveness of pre-trained Transformer based language models in retrieving and classifying fake news in a highly specialized domain of COVID-19. Our proposed two stage model performs significantly better than other baseline NLP approaches. Our knowledge base, that we prepare through collecting factual data from reliable sources from the web can be dynamic and change to a large extent, without having to retrain our models again for as long as the distribution is consistent. All of our proposed models can run in near real-time with moderately inexpensive compute. Our work is based on the assumption that our knowledge base is accurate and timely. This assumption might not always be true in a scenario such as COVID-19 where "facts" are changing as we learn more about the virus and its effects. Therefore a more systematic approach is needed for retrieving and classifying claims using this dynamic knowledge base. Our future work consists of weighting our knowledge base on the basis of the duration of the claims and benchmarking each claim against novel sources of ground truth.

Our model performance can be further boosted by better pre-training, through domain specific knowledge. In one of the more recent work by (Guo et al., 2020), the authors propose a novel semantic textual similarity dataset specific to COVID-19. Pre-training our models using such specific datasets could help in better understanding of the domain and ultimately better performance.

Fake news and misinformation is an increasingly important and a difficult problem to solve, especially in an unforeseen situation like the COVID-19 pandemic. Leveraging state of the art machine learning and deep learning algorithms along with preparation and curation of novel datasets can help address the challenge of fake news related to COVID-19 and other public health crises.

## References


Meni Adler, Jonathan Berant, and Ido Dagan. 2012. Entailment-based text exploration with application to the health-care domain. In *Proceedings of the ACL 2012 System Demonstrations*, pages 79–84.

Steven Bird, Ewan Klein, and Edward Loper. 2009. *Natural language processing with Python: analyzing text with the natural language toolkit.* " O'Reilly Media, Inc.".

Joseph Bullock, Katherine Hoffmann Pham, Cynthia Sin Nga Lam, Miguel Luengo-Oroz, et al. 2020. Mapping the landscape of artificial intelligence applications against covid-19. *arXiv preprint arXiv:2003.11336.*

Qian Chen, Xiaodan Zhu, Zhen-Hua Ling, Diana Inkpen, and Si Wei. 2017. Neural natural language inference models enhanced with external knowledge. *arXiv preprint arXiv:1711.04289.*

Nick Craswell. 2009. Mean reciprocal rank. *Encyclopedia of database systems*, 1703.

Ido Dagan, Dan Roth, Mark Sammons, and Fabio Massimo Zanzotto. 2013. Recognizing textual entailment: Models and applications. *Synthesis Lectures on Human Language Technologies*, 6(4):1–220.

Richard Davis and Chris Proctor. 2017. Fake news, real consequences: Recruiting neural networks for the fight against fake news.

Jacob Devlin, Ming-Wei Chang, Kenton Lee, and Kristina Toutanova. 2018. Bert: Pre-training of deep bidirectional transformers for language understanding. *arXiv preprint arXiv:1810.04805.*

Riccardo Gallotti, Francesco Valle, Nicola Castaldo, Pierluigi Sacco, and Manlio De Domenico. 2020. Assessing the risks of" infodemics" in response to covid-19 epidemics. *arXiv preprint arXiv:2004.03997.*

Xiao Guo, Hengameh Mirzaalian, Ekraam Sabir, Aysush Jaiswal, and Wael Abd-Almageed. 2020. Cord19sts: Covid-19 semantic textual similarity dataset. *arXiv preprint arXiv:2007.02461.*

Andreas Hanselowski, Avinesh PVS, Benjamin Schiller, Felix Caspelherr, Debanjan Chaudhuri, Christian M Meyer, and Iryna Gurevych. 2018. A retrospective analysis of the fake news challenge stance detection task. *arXiv preprint arXiv:1806.05180.*

Michiel Hermans and Benjamin Schrauwen. 2013. Training and analysing deep recurrent neural networks. In *Advances in neural information processing systems*, pages 190–198.

Heejung Jwa, Dongsuk Oh, Kinam Park, Jang Mook Kang, and Heuiseok Lim. 2019. exbake: Automatic fake news detection model based on bidirectional encoder representations from transformers (bert). *Applied Sciences*, 9(19):4062.

Diederik P Kingma and Jimmy Ba. 2014. Adam: A method for stochastic optimization. *arXiv preprint arXiv:1412.6980.*

Zhenzhong Lan, Mingda Chen, Sebastian Goodman, Kevin Gimpel, Piyush Sharma, and Radu Soricut. 2019. Albert: A lite bert for self-supervised learning of language representations. *arXiv preprint arXiv:1909.11942.*

Yuri Malheiros, Alan Moraes, Cleyton Trindade, and Silvio Meira. 2012. A source code recommender system to support newcomers. In *2012 IEEE 36th Annual Computer Software and Applications Conference*, pages 19–24. IEEE.

Yelena Mejova, Ingmar Weber, and Luis Fernandez-Luque. 2018. Online health monitoring using facebook advertisement audience estimates in the united states: evaluation study. *JMIR public health and surveillance*, 4(1):e30.

Wim Naudé. 2020. Artificial intelligence against covid-19: An early review.

Yixin Nie, Haonan Chen, and Mohit Bansal. 2019. Combining fact extraction and verification with neural semantic matching networks. In *Proceedings of the AAAI Conference on Artificial Intelligence*, volume 33, pages 6859–6866.

Jeffrey Pennington, Richard Socher, and Christopher D Manning. 2014. Glove: Global vectors for word representation. In *Proceedings of the 2014 conference on empirical methods in natural language processing (EMNLP)*, pages 1532–1543.

Matthew E. Peters, Mark Neumann, Mohit Iyyer, Matt Gardner, Christopher Clark, Kenton Lee, and Luke Zettlemoyer. 2018. Deep contextualized word representations. In *Proc. of NAACL.*

Benjamin Riedel, Isabelle Augenstein, Georgios P Spithourakis, and Sebastian Riedel. 2017. A simple but tough-to-beat baseline for the fake news challenge stance detection task. *arXiv preprint arXiv:1707.03264.*

Zhiqing Sun, Hongkun Yu, Xiaodan Song, Renjie Liu, Yiming Yang, and Denny Zhou. 2020. Mobilebert: a compact task-agnostic bert for resource-limited devices. *arXiv preprint arXiv:2004.02984.*

James Thorne, Andreas Vlachos, Christos Christodoulopoulos, and Arpit Mittal. 2018. Fever: a large-scale dataset for fact extraction and verification. *arXiv preprint arXiv:1803.05355.*

Ashish Vaswani, Noam Shazeer, Niki Parmar, Jakob Uszkoreit, Llion Jones, Aidan N Gomez, Łukasz Kaiser, and Illia Polosukhin. 2017. Attention is all you need. In *Advances in neural information processing systems*, pages 5998–6008.

Alex Wang, Amanpreet Singh, Julian Michael, Felix Hill, Omer Levy, and Samuel R Bowman. 2018. Glue: A multi-task benchmark and analysis platform for natural language understanding. *arXiv preprint arXiv:1804.07461.*

# Measuring Alignment to Authoritarian State Media as Framing Bias

**Timothy Niven**
Doublethink Lab
Taipei, Taiwan
tim@doublethinklab.org

**Hung-Yu Kao**
Intelligent Knowledge Management Lab
National Cheng Kung University
Tainan, Taiwan
hykao@mail.ncku.edu.tw

## Abstract

We introduce what is to the best of our knowledge a new task in natural language processing: measuring alignment to authoritarian state media. We operationalize alignment in terms of sociological definitions of media bias. We take as a case study the alignment of four Taiwanese media outlets to the Chinese Communist Party state media. We present the results of an initial investigation using the frequency of words in psychologically meaningful categories. Our findings suggest that the chosen word categories correlate with framing choices. We develop a calculation method that yields reasonable results for measuring alignment, agreeing well with the known labels. We confirm that our method does capture event selection bias, but whether it captures framing bias requires further investigation.

## 1 Introduction

Information warfare is of increasing concern in the current era, persecuted through various channels. Recently, social media has become a key focus, however traditional media continues to play an important role. As Cook (2020) notes, the economically powerful authoritarian Chinese Communist Party (CCP) is rapidly expanding its influence over media production and distribution channels globally, and is applying tactics developed for co-opting the Chinese diaspora in different countries to local mainstream media.

The scale of CCP investment may also signify the importance they attach to the role of traditional media (Cook, 2020). There have been some apparent successes. For example, a recent study significantly correlated access to CCP state media in Africa with favourable views of the CCP-state (Bailard, 2016). On the other hand, CCP media is not considered to be nearly as successful in the West. As an authoritarian party-state, CCP-branded media suffers from a large credibility deficit. As Varral (2020) notes, at China Global Television Network (CGTN) it is generally accepted internally that CGTN's influence is not what is could be given the amount of funding they receive. Nevertheless, given the scale of investment, it is possible that CCP state media are learning from their mistakes, refining their messaging, and iteratively improving their ability to influence foreign nations.

Of equal concern are efforts to overcome the key branding issue. As detailed by Brady (2017), the CCP's media strategy has long included the policy of "borrowing a boat to go on the ocean": strategic partnerships with foreign media organizations to spread their messaging. A recent example is advertorial agreements with Western media such as The Washington Post to run a China Daily supplement in their own newspapers (albeit with a small warning label). Such agreements allow the CCP to shake off their own brand and borrow from the credibility carefully developed by such newspapers. The "borrow a boat" policy has also been augmented with the "buy a boat" policy: strategic mergers and acquisitions of foreign media assets (Brady, 2017).





*Proceedings of the 3rd NLP4IF Workshop on NLP for Internet Freedom*, pages 11–21
Barcelona, Spain (Online), December 12, 2020

For example, Auckland's only Chinese-language 24-hour radio station, FM 90.6, was taken over by a subsidiary of China Radio International (CRI), and now sources all its news from CRI and its Australian subsidiary (Brady, 2017). With a bought and paid for boat, audiences do not even have the luxury of a small warning label on the content. Related to this last category are media outlets that are owned by agents loyal to the CCP, either ideologically or financially motivated. A prime example is Taiwan's *China Times*, a company of the Want-Want group who are proudly aligned to the CCP.[1]

Advertorial supplements from *China Daily*, subsidiaries of CCP state media, and media outlets run by loyal agents of the CCP are examples of *alignment* to authoritarian state media, the focus of our work. We define such alignment as effectively acting as an agent of that state: spreading their messaging, and working towards their goals. Alignment in this sense can therefore pertain to agents (media outlets or journalists), and also to text (news articles).

In our work with civil society organizations and journalists around the world, we have identified the usefulness of an NLP tool to detect and track media that are aligned to the CCP. The primacy of investigative journalism is not in question. In many cases the alignment of agents can be established by investigating the people and companies involved. However, such an NLP tool could be helpful in a number of ways. It could flag new and emerging media for investigation. It could detect the point in time when a media organization undergoes change in the bias of its content (which may be coincidental, for example, with when it was purchased by another company, flagging the company for investigation). It could be used to compare CCP influence across countries and time. It could hopefully also give insight into how the alignment is expressed - e.g., what issues and framings are important - which may help to understand the evolving nature of CCP information operations. Finally, it would ideally be able to provide hard statistical evidence to support claims of bias.

From an NLP perspective, this research problem is novel (as far as we are aware). Yet by operationalizing alignment in terms of media bias we are able to draw upon a wealth of prior research. Our conceptualization of media bias follows the sociological model reported in Hamborg (2018). The types of bias we intend to address concern what is reported, and how it is reported. What is (and is not) reported is covered by *event selection bias*. How it is reported is covered by *word choice*, *labeling*, and *framing bias*. In this work we aim to measure framing bias, and find that our methodology also captures event selection bias. We ideally want an unsupervised solution that is applicable to as many languages (and therefore national contexts) as possible.

In the abstract, our methodology is to treat the CCP state media data as a "propaganda distribution." As news outlets in other countries will follow their own news cycle and political context, we need a way to factor out this part of their observed distribution. We then check the remainder for alignment in the direction of the CCP propaganda distribution.

In the present work, we concretely implement this methodology by using the frequencies of words in psychologically meaningful lexical categories drawn from the Linguistic Inquiry and Word Count (LIWC) dictionary (Pennebaker et al., 2015). We identify 15 categories that appear to relate to framing. For each chosen category, we calculate an indicator variable representing whether a media outlet differs from the Taiwanese mean in the direction of the CCP, and take the average of these indicators as a score. Our results are a strong match for the expected labels, and also capture the ideological leaning of the four Taiwanese media outlets studied. We therefore have reasonable confidence that our methodology captures the known bias in the data. However, an initial qualitative study is inconclusive regarding whether we have captured framing bias. We do, however, confirm that our methodology unexpectedly captures event selection bias. Therefore, a careful analysis of framing in our dataset should be conducted to confirm the nature of the bias our method is capturing.

[1]For example, consider this editorial in support of the annexation of Taiwan by the CCP-state: https://www.chinatimes.com/newspapers/20200524000371-260108?chdtv.

## 2 Related Work

Gentzkow and Shapiro (2006) offer one of the earliest computational methods for measuring framing bias in the U.S. national media context. They use the $\chi^2$ statistic to compare the frequency of phrases used by Republicans and Democrats, selecting the top-$k$ phrases for each as marking the bias distributions. We implemented this method on our data, but found it captured more differences in national contexts than ideological differences (e.g. "report from Beijing"). We therefore hypothesize that this methodology is not suitable for international bias measurements unless augmented by some other technique for factoring out national differences.

Field (2018) develop a multilingual method for detecting frames based on the coding in the Media Frames Corpus (Card et al., 2016). Their methodology could ostensibly be used to study international framing bias. They collected frame-specific lexicons in English using the PMI of words with the annotated frames, then translated the lexicons into the target language, using word embeddings to refine the lexicon through query expansion so as to more accurately capture the local linguistic and political context. Our experiments with this methodology did not prove as successful as our reported methodology, yielding more variable and noisy results. It is possible that the lexicon construction process is too noisy for our purpose. We also suspect that using a pre-defined set of high-level frames is not sensitive enough. It is possible that our method of using word categories that relate to framing as opposed to the high-level frames themselves is more flexible, allowing unannotated framings to be expressed in the relative frequencies of lower-level word categories.

Shahid et al. (2020) follow an approach most similar to ours, using the Moral Foundations dictionary (Graham et al., 2013) to analyze framing bias in an unsupervised manner. Their results appear reasonable, and are supported by other studies that suggest the usefulness of moral foundations in understanding framing bias (Fulgoni et al., 2016). One advantage of LIWC is that, to the best of our knowledge, it has been translated into more languages than the Moral Foundations dictionary. Our experience is that lexicon quality is important. Nevertheless, comparing our method to a Chinese version of the Moral Foundations dictionary is necessary future work.

More recent work has considered multi-label and multi-lingual frame detection in a few-shot setting with minimal labeled data (Akyürek et al., 2020). However, their data comes solely from articles about gun violence in the U.S. and also uses a pre-defined set of framings.

A fairly comprehensive plan for research into automated framing bias detection is offered by Hamborg (2020). However, this methodology still involves upstream inaccuracies and components of supervised learning - e.g., aligning entity mentions through coreference resolution. Although we support this research direction as well principled and promising, our initial investigation aims to be fully unsupervised for two reasons. The first is to avoid propagation of upstream errors as much as possible.[2] Second, due to our desire to work with as many languages (and therefore national contexts) as possible, we want to reduce our reliance on language specific resources such as supervised coreference resolution classifiers.

Cremisini et al. (2019) released a dataset for analyzing bias in coverage of the Ukranian crisis including a range of media outlets from 43 countries. Including Russian state media also makes this work closer to our task of measuring alignment to authoritarian state media, although it only deals with a single issue. Application of our methodology to this dataset remains as future work.

The present work complements our existing work on CCP information operations (Tseng and Shen, 2020). The development of our tool could assist this research by identifying local agents (e.g. journalists, influencers) working on behalf of the CCP, which have been found to be an important component of CCP information warfare directed against Taiwan.

[2]As Chinese text does not separate words with a space, the first step in any NLP pipeline is deciding where to draw word boundaries. There is no perfect solution available, so a degree of upstream noise is inevitable, but does not appear crucial for our methodology.

| Media Outlet | Label | Num. Documents | Num. Tokens |
|---|---|---|---|
| China Internet Information Center | CCP state Media | 65,804 | 45,203,219 |
| China Daily | CCP state Media | 6,190 | 4,877,458 |
| China Development Gateway | CCP state Media | 544 | 487,252 |
| China Times (CCP) | CCP state Media | 543 | 632,425 |
| Global Times | CCP state Media | 24,585 | 15,263,884 |
| National Party Media Information Public Platform | CCP state Media | 39,556 | 23,431,048 |
| Xinhua | CCP state Media | 806 | 751,059 |
| People's Daily | CCP state Media | 102,158 | 64,067,371 |
| Qiushi | CCP state Media | 3,210 | 3,063,152 |
| China Times (Taiwan) | Aligned to CCP | 17,143 | 5,790,180 |
| United Daily | Bias Towards CCP | 17,275 | 6,137,210 |
| Liberty Times | Bias Against CCP | 6,704 | 2,015,226 |
| Apple Daily | Oppose CCP | 6,076 | 1,864,850 |

Table 1: The composition of our dataset. The label for Taiwan's *China Times* is well established, making it a good test case for our method. *United Daily* can be roughly considered ideologically closer to the CCP, but independent. *Liberty Times* can be considered ideologically opposed to the CCP. *Apple Daily* is a staunch opponent of the CCP. Note that the data we collected is filtered by a large list of keywords relating to politics.

## 3 Data

We scraped news articles from the media outlets listed in Table 1 from January 1st, 2020, to May 1st, 2020. The scraping process filtered for content related to politics using a large manually curated list of keywords. The outlets labeled CCP state media provide the "propaganda distribution" for bias calculations. We consider the articles from all CCP state media domains as a single distribution.[3] The Taiwanese media fall into three categories. First, we have Taiwan's *China Times* which is known to be working on behalf of the CCP. The three other domains provide coverage of the rest of the ideological spectrum: *United Daily* is ideologically closer to the CCP yet independent; *Liberty Times* is ideologically opposed to the CCP; *Apple Daily* is a staunch opponent.

For all media domains, we manually clean the scraped text to remove common template tokens, such as journalist credits and advertising. Word segmentation is then performed with jieba[4] augmented with the custom dictionary provided by Media Cloud (Chuang et al., 2014).[5]

## 4 Methodology

In this section we first motivate our use of LIWC categories, and our method of selecting which categories reliably relate to framing. We then outline our calculation method and procedure for statistical inference.

### 4.1 LIWC Categories and Framing

The psychologically meaningful word categories we use come from LIWC dictionary (Pennebaker et al., 2015). The LIWC dictionary has been carefully developed over a decade and a half and has been used in many psycholinguistic studies. We use the 2015 versions of the simplified and traditional Chinese LIWC dictionaries (Huang et al., 2012). Even though China and Taiwan share a common language, there are many important linguistic differences. Fortunately, these dictionaries were developed appropriately for their respective linguistic contexts, and represent more than a naive mapping between traditional and simplified characters.[6] Altogether there are 79 word categories from which we select 15 that appear to relate to framing.

[3]Future work is to investigate each outlet separately and pick apart what parts of the propaganda distribution they are responsible for.

[4]https://github.com/fxsjy/jieba

[5]https://github.com/berkmancenter/mediacloud

[6]The mean Jaccard similarity of the 79 word category sets across the two dictionaries is 0.88, with 0.15 standard deviation.

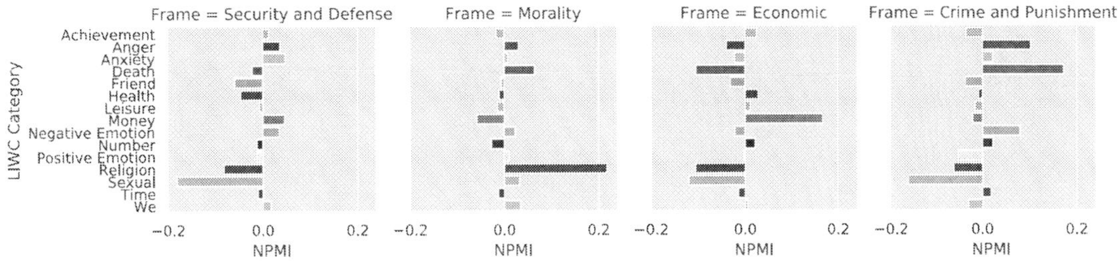


Figure 1: The NPMI of the 15 LIWC categories we selected with the annotated framings in the Media Frames corpus. These relationships appear reasonable and underwrite our assumption that the frequencies of using these categories in news articles express framing choices.

Similar to the methodology of Field et al. (2018), we consider the normalized Pointwise Mutual Information (NPMI) of LIWC categories with the annotated frames of the Media Frames corpus (Card et al., 2016). In order to account for document length, we consider the event space in terms of the selection of individual words. For each document, we consider all its words to be associated with all frames ascribed by the annotators. Let $x_f$ be the event that a word appears with a frame, $f$. Let $y_c$ be the event that the selected word comes from an LIWC category, $c$. The NPMI of $c$ with $f$ is then calculated in the standard way as

$$\text{NPMI}(c, f) = \frac{\log(p(y_c|x_f)/p(x_f))}{-\log_2(p(x_f, y_c))}, \tag{1}$$

where the denominator is self-information.

The LIWC dictionary involves some 79 word categories. Experiments with every word category did not yield meaningful results. It was therefore reasonable to hypothesize that only a subset of the LIWC categories are reliably associated with framing. Observing the NPMI values, we decided to choose a 0.01 absolute NPMI cutoff value with any framing, resulting in 15 categories. Figure 1 shows the NPMI of the chosen categories with a subset of frames. These results are inherently reasonable, which motivates their use in framing analysis. Some findings of note: the "Religion" category almost singularly defines the "Morality" frame in the same way that "Money" defines the "Economic" frame. It is expected that "Anxiety" and "Negative Emotion" are well correlated with "Security and Defense," and that "Death" and "Anger" are most associated with "Crime and Punishment." Given these results, we view this subset of LIWC categories as correlates of framing. We hypothesize that the stable and meaningful results we achieve, as outlined below, in part come from the flexibility of modeling framing with respect to these more general word categories. We now turn to describe our calculation method for framing bias.

### 4.2 Calculation Method

For a specific country, our methodology scores how often a media outlet deviates from the national mean of that country in the direction of the CCP. Formally, the CCP distribution is defined by chosen media outlets, $m_{\text{ccp}}^{(i)}$, in the set, $\mathcal{M}_{\text{ccp}}$, where $i = 1, 2, \ldots, |\mathcal{M}_{\text{ccp}}|$. These are to be compared to the national media outlets, $m_{\text{national}}^{(j)}$, in the set $\mathcal{M}_{\text{national}}$, where $j = 1, 2, \ldots, |\mathcal{M}_{\text{national}}|$. The media outlets under consideration are listed in Table 1.

We first calculate the mean frequencies of each LIWC category $c \in \mathcal{C}$ per document in the corpus collected for the CCP media outlets. Let $\mathcal{D}_{\text{ccp}}$ be the collection documents from all media outlets in $\mathcal{M}_{\text{ccp}}$. Let $F^{(c)}(d)$ be a function that counts the proportion of words from category $c$ in document $d$. Then the CCP's mean is:

$$\mu_{\text{ccp}}^{(c)} = \frac{1}{|\mathcal{D}_{\text{ccp}}|} \sum_{d \in \mathcal{D}_{\text{ccp}}} F^{(c)}(d). \tag{2}$$

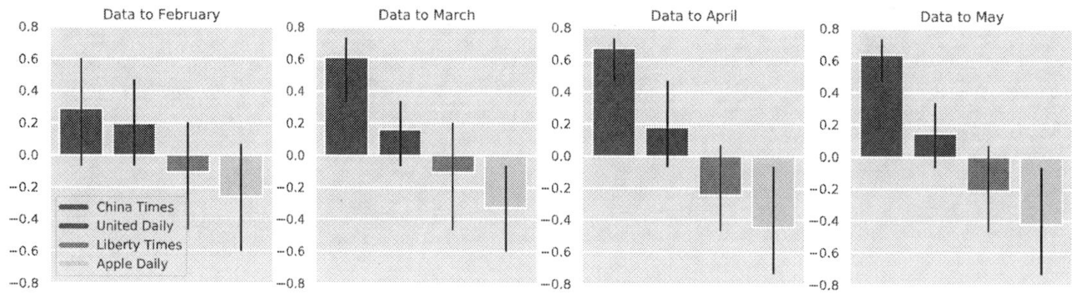


Figure 2: Results of our scoring calculation (Equation 5). Error bars represent 95% confidence intervals for the score given the bootstrap distributions. The data starts from January 1st, 2020, and continues to the first of the indicated month. After one month the results are uncertain, with all error bars crossing zero. By month two the results have already settled down into the qualitative pattern we expect, with *China Times* singled out as aligned to the CCP state media. The results for the other three media outlets also qualitatively align with our expectations given the known ideologies of each.

We calculate the means for the national context similarly, but remove the media outlet under consideration from the set in order to stop outliers from having an oversized impact on the mean (as it is outliers we want to detect, this increases the sensitivity of our method). Let $\mathcal{D}_{national/m}$ be the set of documents for all $m \in \mathcal{M}_{\text{national}/m}$. Then the national mean is:

$$\mu^{(c)}_{\text{national}/m} = \frac{1}{|\mathcal{D}_{\text{national}/m}|} \sum_{d \in \mathcal{D}_{\text{national}/m}} F^{(c)}(d). \tag{3}$$

The final ingredient in our score is the category means for the media outlet under investigation, $m$. Let $\mathcal{D}_m$ be the set of documents for $m$. Then the mean is:

$$\mu^{(c)}_m = \frac{1}{|\mathcal{D}_m|} \sum_{d \in \mathcal{D}_m} F^{(c)}(d). \tag{4}$$

Our final bias score for $m$, $s_m$, is then the average number of categories for which the difference from the national mean is in the direction of the CCP:

$$s_m = \frac{1}{|\mathcal{C}|} \sum_{c \in \mathcal{C}} \mathbb{1}\left[\text{sign}(\mu^{(c)}_{\text{national}/m} - \mu^{(c)}_m) = \text{sign}(\mu^{(c)}_{\text{national}/m} - \mu^{(c)}_{\text{ccp}})\right] \tag{5}$$

### 4.3 Statistical Inference

We favour non-parametric statistical inference through bootstrapping (Efron and Tibshirani, 1986). Specifically, as our data involves a time series, we use the tapered block bootstrap (Kunsch, 1989) in order to preserve the dynamics of the news cycle through time. We use the python implementation provided by the recombinator package.[7]

## 5 Results

For each domain to be scored, we perform 1,000 bootstrap samplings of the whole dataset, and report the distribution of results. The 95% confidence interval is calculated in terms of percentiles of the bootstrap distribution. We are interested to know how stable the results are with varying amounts of data. We therefore repeat the bootstrap scoring procedure with varying time periods. All scores start at the January 1st, 2020, and extend an integer number

[7]https://github.com/InvestmentSystems/recombinator

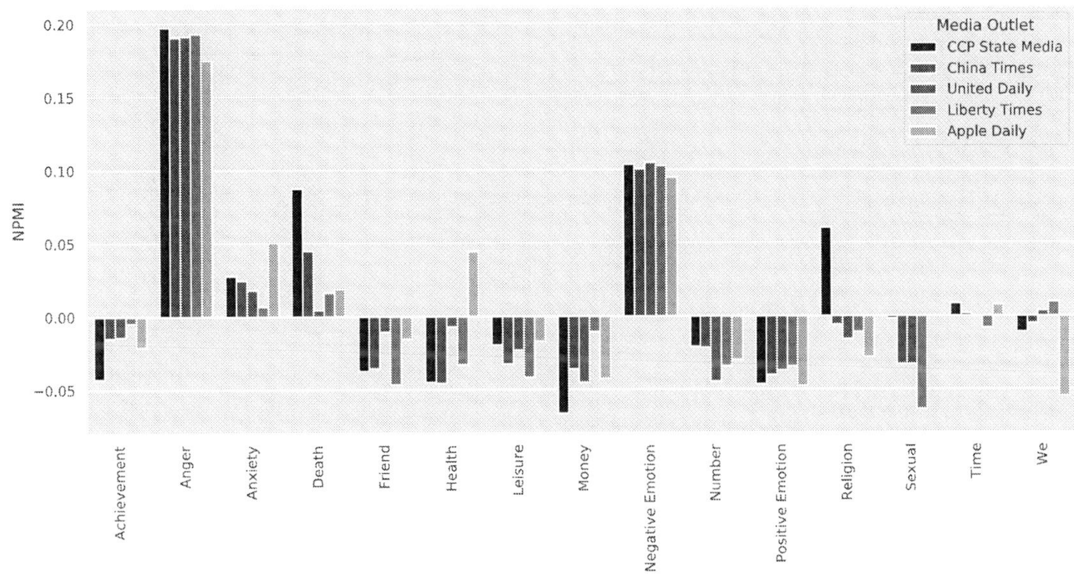


Figure 3: NPMI of LIWC categories with sentences including the word "protest." It stands out that the CCP prefers the *Death* and *Religion* categories. Randomly sampling 20 sentences with "protest" and these categories reveals that when the CCP report on protest in our dataset, they discuss murder, crime, and damage to property. However, they also talk about protests in the US, suggesting that this statistical signal is also picking up event selection bias.

of months, up to May 1st, 2020. Figure 2 shows the results. With two months of data the expected qualitative pattern is observed: *China Times* is strongly aligned to the CCP, the lower bound of the confidence interval well above zero; *United Daily* is independent but ideologically closer; *Liberty Times* is ideologically divergent; *Apple Daily* is strongly divergent from the CCP. The pattern appears to be stabilizing over time.

**Limitations:** Although the results appear to be stabilizing, we believe this length of time is still short enough to leave uncertainty about the reliability of our methodology. The results should also be reproduced in different national and linguistic contexts for more thorough verification.

## 6 Analysis

Our results suggest we have measured bias in our dataset in accordance with the expected labels. However, our case that we have captured framing bias rests on the findings of Section 4.1: that the LIWC categories we chose correlate well with the annotations in the Media Frames corpus. This case needs to be strengthened by a careful look at frames in our data. We conducted a cursory analysis that is suggestive yet inconclusive about framing bias. However, it does confirm that our methodology captures event selection bias.

We identified sentences that include at least one instance of the word "protest." We then calculated the NPMI of LIWC categories with these sentences following equation (1), however at the sentence not document level.[8] The distribution over LIWC categories is given in Figure 3. We observe that the CCP prefers the categories "Death" and "Religion" compared to Taiwanese media (with *China Times* biasing in their direction). Given how these categories correlate with frames as observed in Figure 1, these would appear to indicate the CCP frames protest in terms of "Crime and Punishment" and "Morality" in our dataset. To check this hypothesis, we

[8]We found the document level did not yield reasonable results, which is to be expected, as a document can discuss a number of topics and concepts. Furthermore, some CCP state media have the habit of reporting a number of different news items in a single document.

| Media Outlet | $p$(America) | $p$(Protest) | $p$(America\|Protest) |
|---|---|---|---|
| CCP state Media | 0.094 | 0.007 | 0.410 |
| China Times (Taiwan) | 0.091 | 0.018 | 0.140 |
| United Daily | 0.106 | 0.025 | 0.048 |
| Liberty Times | 0.069 | 0.019 | 0.082 |
| Apple Daily | 0.098 | 0.043 | 0.036 |

Table 2: Statistics of coverage of "America" and "Protest" in our dataset. The CCP is far less likely to discuss protest, but when they do, they talk about protests in the U.S. almost half the time. The *China Times* strongly biases in this direction relative to the Taiwanese mean. If a media outlet follows CCP frames, we would expect our methodology to also indirectly capture event selection bias.

randomly sampled 20 sentences containing "protest" for inspection. We observed that most of the sentences are indeed about murder, death, and criminal behavior, and some highlight the negative impacts of protest on society. However, to fully address this question a more principled analysis of framing conducted by political scientists is required.

We also observed that the majority of these sentences were about protests in the United States after the murder of George Floyd. We therefore hypothesized that we are also measuring event selection bias. Table 2 shows the statistics of covering "America" and "protest" in our dataset, calculated as any document with at least one sentence mentioning either, or both. We observe that, while the CCP is far less likely to discuss protest than the Taiwanese media, when they do, it is nearly half the time about protest in the United States. *China Times* strongly biases in this direction, relative to the Taiwanese distribution. It is reasonable to suggest that, if a media outlet follows CCP framing on a specific issue, detection of similar framing over a period of time may also indirectly capture event selection bias. We leave a more thorough investigation of this question to future work.

## 7 Conclusion

We are surprised by how well our calculation method matches the known bias labels. Lexical category approaches have some well known difficulties, particularly that they do not consider syntax - e.g., a negative emotion word following a negation may not express negative emotion. Furthermore, it may be that following CCP framing does not necessarily represent the CCP's interests in different national contexts. We observe an example of this: the *China Times* uses "we" in sentences containing "China" far more than any other Taiwanese newspaper - but the CCP state media does not. Despite these complications, with enough data our methodology appears to work qualitatively well and yield stable results. Drilling down to consider framing around specific issues also appears to yield qualitatively reasonable insights consistent with our expectations. Our hypothesis is therefore that the aforementioned complications are effectively smoothed over by enough data.

Our assumption that the LIWC categories capture framing, and therefore that our methodology captures framing bias, is based on the observation of meaningful correlations of these categories with the annotations in the Media Frames corpus. However, we also saw in our qualitative analysis that we are picking up event selection bias. A closer examination will be necessary to establish the extent to which our calculation method is picking up framing and event selection bias. It will be necessary to observe data over a longer period of time in order to validate the observed stability of our conclusions. We must also be apply it to different linguistic and national contexts, over many more media organizations. We should also compare our methodology to another apparent correlate of framing: the Moral Foundations Dictionary. The LIWC resource is also a constraint on the number of languages we can handle. Currently there are 15 languages covered by LIWC. Therefore, future work is to find a way to cover more languages, ideally in an unsupervised manner that does not rely on such resources.

Our calculation method is very simple, and can almost certainly be improved. For example, we have found that using vectors of our chosen LIWC category frequencies and taking the first principal component also yields a surprisingly coherent ideological ordering of media, including the different CCP state media outlets. Vector-based calculation methods are likely to be more sensitive to the statistics than our binary indicator variables, and may also facilitate more complicated calculations, such as comparing to multiple, different propaganda distributions. It also makes more sense to consider frames as occupying regions in the 15-dimensional space of frequencies induced by our LIWC category selections (see Figure 1), as opposed to considering the categories separately.

How might our methodology be applied to other authoritarian states? Our results suggest that collecting two months of data from the authoritarian state media, and from media outlets of interest with unknown labels, should be enough to apply our scoring calculation. It will be interesting to explore other potential applications of our methodology, such as detection of content farms (Tseng and Shen, 2020), or networks of Twitter accounts operated by the CCP. We make our code publicly available to facilitate subsequent research.[9]

In the introduction we outlined a number of goals for the NLP tool we have set out to build. How does our methodology help to those ends? With two months of data we could tag an emerging or unknown media outlet as potentially part of CCP information operations. We have not modeled the time dimension so far, so we could not detect when a media outlet undergoes a change in alignment. We could compare the media outlets within and across countries, but not across time. Drilling down around specific concepts, events, or entities does facilitate analysis of how alignment is expressed, as our analysis of protest suggests. Our calculation method can be considered a form of statistical evidence, however should be further validated as outlined above.

We note an important weakness in our methodology. Taking the difference from the average national media will fail where the national media is almost entirely aligned to the CCP. For example, it is estimated that in Australia 95% of the Chinese language media is under CCP influence (Munro and Wen, 2016). A similar situation exists in New Zealand (Brady, 2017). In such contexts our methodology would require modification. It would be most desirable to seek a more absolute measure of alignment, but it may be difficult to develop one that is automatic and works in every national political context.

For future work, we intend to explore the use of word embeddings with techniques developed in the gender bias literature to try and identify directions in the CCP state media embedding space that capture the propaganda distribution. Initial experiments are promising. For example, the distance between "Taiwan" and "country" is much larger in the CCP embedding space then in the Taiwan (minus *China Times*) embedding space, with *China Times* falling quite far outside the Taiwanese distribution in the direction of the CCP.[10] It may be possible to build a list from official CCP framings of particular issues such as Taiwan (Brady, 2015). However, such a static approach would be less ideal than one that could be automatically learned and updated daily. We leave these challenges for future work.

## Acknowledgements

We would like to thank the reviewers for their highly useful feedback.

## References

Afra Feyza Akyürek, Lei Guo, Randa Elanwar, Prakash Ishwar, Margrit Betke, and Derry Tanti Wijaya. 2020. Multi-label and multilingual news framing analysis. In *Proceedings of the 58th Annual Meeting of the Association for Computational Linguistics*, pages 8614–8624, Online, July. Association for Computational Linguistics.

[9]https://github.com/doublethinklab/nlp4if2020p

[10]Comparing distances in different embedding spaces is know to be problematic (Gonen et al., 2020), however we offer this result as suggestive.

Catie Snow Bailard. 2016. China in africa: An analysis of the effect of chinese media expansion on african public opinion. *The International Journal of Press/Politics*, 21(4):446–471.

Anne-Marie Brady. 2015. Unifying the ancestral land: The ccp's "taiwan" frames. *The China Quarterly*, 223:787–806.

Anne-Marie Brady. 2017. Magic weapons: China's political influence activities under xi jinping.

Dallas Card, Justin Gross, Amber Boydstun, and Noah A. Smith. 2016. Analyzing framing through the casts of characters in the news. In *Proceedings of the 2016 Conference on Empirical Methods in Natural Language Processing*, pages 1410–1420, Austin, Texas, November. Association for Computational Linguistics.

Jason Chuang, Sands Fish, David Larochelle, William P. Li, and Rebecca Weiss. 2014. Large-scale topical analysis of multiple online news sources with media cloud.

Sarah Cook. 2020. Beijing's global megaphone: The expansion of chinese communist party media influence since 2017. Retrieved August 26 2020 from https://freedomhouse.org/report/special-report/2020/beijings-global-megaphone.

Andres Cremisini, Daniela Aguilar, and Mark A. Finlayson. 2019. A challenging dataset for bias detection: The case of the crisis in the ukraine. In Robert Thomson, Halil Bisgin, Christopher Dancy, and Ayaz Hyder, editors, *Social, Cultural, and Behavioral Modeling*, pages 173–183, Cham. Springer International Publishing.

Bradley Efron and Robert Tibshirani. 1986. Bootstrap methods for standard errors, confidence intervals, and other measures of statistical accuracy. *Statist. Sci.*, 1(1):54–75, 02.

Anjalie Field, Doron Kliger, Shuly Wintner, Jennifer Pan, Dan Jurafsky, and Yulia Tsvetkov. 2018. Framing and agenda-setting in russian news: a computational analysis of intricate political strategies. *CoRR*, abs/1808.09386.

Dean Fulgoni, Jordan Carpenter, Lyle Ungar, and Daniel Preoţiuc-Pietro. 2016. An empirical exploration of moral foundations theory in partisan news sources. In *Proceedings of the Tenth International Conference on Language Resources and Evaluation (LREC'16)*, pages 3730–3736, Portorož, Slovenia, May. European Language Resources Association (ELRA).

Matthew Gentzkow and Jesse M Shapiro. 2006. What drives media slant? evidence from u.s. daily newspapers. Working Paper 12707, National Bureau of Economic Research, November.

Hila Gonen, Ganesh Jawahar, Djamé Seddah, and Yoav Goldberg. 2020. Simple, interpretable and stable method for detecting words with usage change across corpora. In *Proceedings of the 58th Annual Meeting of the Association for Computational Linguistics*, pages 538–555, Online, July. Association for Computational Linguistics.

Jesse Graham, Jonathan Haidt, Sena Koleva, Matt Motyl, Ravi Iyer, Sean P. Wojcik, and Peter H. Ditto. 2013. Moral foundations theory. In *Advances in Experimental Social Psychology*, pages 55–130. Elsevier.

Felix Hamborg, Karsten Donnay, and Bela Gipp. 2018. Automated identification of media bias in news articles: an interdisciplinary literature review. *International Journal on Digital Libraries*, pages 1–25.

Felix Hamborg. 2020. Media bias, the social sciences, and NLP: Automating frame analyses to identify bias by word choice and labeling. In *Proceedings of the 58th Annual Meeting of the Association for Computational Linguistics: Student Research Workshop*, pages 79–87, Online, July. Association for Computational Linguistics.

Chin-Lan Huang, Cindy K Chung, N. Hui, Yi-Cheng Lin, Yi-Tai Seih, Wei-Chuan Chen, Ben C. P. Lam, Michael H. Bond, and J. W. Pennebaker. 2012. The development of the chinese linguistic inquiry and word count dictionary. *Chinese Journal of Psychology*, 54:185–201.

Hans R. Kunsch. 1989. The jackknife and the bootstrap for general stationary observations. *Ann. Statist.*, 17(3):1217–1241, 09.

Kelsey Munro and Phillip Wen. 2016. Chinese language newspapers in australia: Beijing controls messaging, propaganda in press. Retrieved August 31 2020 from https://www.smh.com.au/national/chinese-language-newspapers-in-australia-beijing-controlsmessaging-propaganda-in-press-20160610-gpg0s3.html.

James Pennebaker, Ryan Boyd, Kayla Jordan, and Kate Blackburn. 2015. The development and psychometric properties of liwc2015. 09.

Usman Shahid, Barbara Di Eugenio, Andrew Rojecki, and Elena Zheleva. 2020. Detecting and understanding moral biases in news. In *Proceedings of the First Joint Workshop on Narrative Understanding, Storylines, and Events*, pages 120–125, Online, July. Association for Computational Linguistics.

Poyu Tseng and Puma Shen. 2020. The chinese infodemic in taiwan. Retrieved October 11 2020 from https://medium.com/doublethinklab/the-chinese-infodemic-in-taiwan-25e9ac3d941e.

Merriden Varrall. 2020. Behind the news: Inside china global television network. Retrieved August 26 2020 from https://www.lowyinstitute.org/publications/behind-news-inside-china-global-television-network.

# Incorporating Count-Based Features into Pre-Trained Models for Improved Stance Detection

**Anushka Prakash**
School of Computer Science
University of Birmingham
United Kingdom
anushkaprakash6@gmail.com

**Harish Tayyar Madabushi**
School of Computer Science
University of Birmingham
United Kingdom
harish@harishtayyarmadabushi.com

## Abstract

The explosive growth and popularity of Social Media has revolutionised the way we communicate and collaborate. Unfortunately, this same ease of accessing and sharing information has led to an explosion of misinformation and propaganda. Given that stance detection can significantly aid in veracity prediction, this work focuses on boosting automated stance detection, a task on which pre-trained models have been extremely successful on, as on several other tasks. This work shows that the task of stance detection can benefit from feature based information, especially on certain under performing classes, however, integrating such features into pre-trained models using ensembling is challenging. We propose a novel architecture for integrating features with pre-trained models that address these challenges and test our method on the RumourEval 2019 dataset. This method achieves state-of-the-art results with an F1-score of 63.94 on the test set.

## 1 Introduction and Motivation

In today's world, it is hard to imagine life without the internet and social media. The exponential growth of social media platforms over the past decade has provided people with an extremely convenient medium to access, consume and disseminate information. Social media has also become the primary source of news due to its ability to allow users to follow real-time updates (Huang et al., 2015). Unfortunately, this has also led to the spread of misinformation and propaganda. A recent example is that of Covid-19 which saw a plethora of misinformation online (Donovon, 2020).

Social media users often have trouble identifying credible resources on various platforms and are frequently guided towards misinformation, causing users to trust misinformation. With about 200 billion tweets posted every day (Krawczyk et al., 2017), manually processing this information to detect rumour can be extremely tedious, time consuming, prone to human error and bias and most importantly impractical. Thus, it is essential to develop efficient automated methods that help in detecting and tracking misinformation online to aid in the fight against misinformation.

There are four primary components to rumour determination: rumour detection, rumour tracking, stance classification, and veracity classification (Zubiaga et al., 2018). Stance classification aims at studying the stance of a reply post (referred to as an 'Opinion') on the source post (referred to as the 'Target' - to what the opinion is subjected). Studies have shown that posts containing false information have a notably higher number of 'denying' replies than the ones that do not (Derczynski et al., 2015). Hence, stance classification can play an important role in assessing the veracity of a rumour.

Given that stance classification can strongly aid in determining the veracity of a post, it is an important if challenging problem to solve. It remains challenging because posts are often sarcastic or witty, while also questioning the validity of the original poster's assumptions or evidence (Hasan and Ng, 2013).

### 1.1 Count-based Features and Pre-Trained models

Recent trends in Natural Language Processing (NLP) have seen the rise of pre-trained language models like GPT (Radford et al., 2018), BERT (Devlin et al., 2019), RoBERTa (Liu et al., 2019) and so on.





*Proceedings of the 3rd NLP4IF Workshop on NLP for Internet Freedom*, pages 22–32
Barcelona, Spain (Online), December 12, 2020

These models are pre-trained on corpora containing millions of words and can be fine-tuned on several tasks to achieve state-of-the-art results. However, it is conceivable that these deep models can benefit from handcrafted features based on human intuition such as an extensive error analysis of these systems' results. For example, early work by Somasundaran and Wiebe (2010) on ideological stance detection observed that a simple unigram model outperformed more complex models using sentiment. This highlights that the stance of a statement is often related to the specific words used to express that opinion (for example, words such as 'Fake', 'Not true', 'disagree' are often used to deny a target claim), and stance classification systems could benefit from explicit features depicting such words. This is especially true when models are used to analyse social media data where elements such as hash tags could have special meaning that can be incorporated using handcrafted features. Furthermore, feature engineering can often be used to boost performances on specific classes that deeper models fail to perform well on. Hence, while it is evident that pre-trained language models have outperformed classical neural networks, simple models trained on hand crafted features can perform well on specific classes or instances that deeper models fail on.

Not only can models designed to analyse social media benefit from the use of handcrafted and count-based features but they are particularly important in handling disinformation and fake news as knowledge of the world at large and global events is required for improved tracking of disinformation. This non-linguistic information is likely to be available through count-based and handcrafted features but not in the pre-trained vector. This is also supported by prior work by Aker et al. (2017) and Bahuleyan and Vechtomova (2017), discussed in Section 2.

Given that handcrafted and count-based features can be used to improve the performance of deep learning models on specific classes or kinds of input, it is natural to ensemble these simple models based on handcrafted features with deeper models such as BERT. However, this is rather challenging for two important reasons:

1. Pre-trained models, such as BERT, are often trained for between 2 and 5 epochs during fine-tuning whereas simpler feature based models need to be trained for much longer. Our experiments show that a simple ensemble of these models results in over-fitting (Section 3.2) .

2. There are likely to be too many features to directly ensemble the raw features with pre-trained models (resulting in too much noise), a loss of important - task specific - information when using dimensionality reduction methods (Section 3.2), and too few output classes to use only the outputs of a feature based model in an ensemble (lack of information).

Therefore, this paper focuses on establishing methods of effectively integrating count-based features into pre-trained models such as BERT and RoBERTa, with specific regard to the identification of disinformation and propaganda on social media, where handcrafted and count-based features can be particularly helpful.

In this work, we formulate stance classification as a multi-class classification problem and experiment with various state-of-the-art NLP techniques to establish the best method of achieving this objective. We use the dataset provided for RumourEval 2019 (Task 7a of SemEval 2019) or the task of stance classification (Gorrell et al., 2019). While tweets have been extensively studied in the past due to their vast reach and brief nature (Krawczyk et al., 2017), this data set also includes posts from Reddit, so focusing on a broader range of social media data. Each conversation thread consists of a source post which states or discusses a rumour. This source post is followed by a set of replies (and replies to these replies) which either 'Support', 'Deny', 'Query' or 'Comment' on the source text (See Figure 1). The source post is also labelled depending on the stance it takes at its (hidden) target (Gorrell et al., 2019).

So as to ensure reproducibility and enable other researchers to build upon this work, we make our program code, hyperparameter details and models available [1].

[1] `https://github.com/Anushka-Prakash/RumourEval-2019-Stance-Detection/`

## 2 Related Work

The effectiveness of stance detection in identifying and tracking misinformation online has led to significant research in this area. This section provides an overview of work related to this study.

Early work on studying perspectives such as that by Lin et al. (2006) use Naïve Bayes and SVM based classifiers to show that word usage alone can help in determining the point of view of a document or sentence. In a similar study, Kim and Hovy (2007) go beyond word usage and exploit the lexical patterns used by people while expressing an opinion. Somasundaran and Wiebe (2010) showed that a unigram based model outperformed a sentiment-based model for determining stance thus reinforcing the importance of words in detecting stance. This shows that the stance of an opinion could be related to the kind of words used to express it. Although working on a different problem set (focused on binary classification) and using different datasets, the above-mentioned studies are relevant to this work because they emphasise on the importance of words used to express an opinion to determine their stance.

Bahuleyan and Vechtomova (2017) hypothesise the presence of certain words in the reply text or the opinion as an indicative measure of its stance. They use these and some tweet specific features like the word count of the tweet to train on a gradient boosting classifier and show that stance classifiers could benefit from these topic independent features. Aker et al. (2017) explore a novel set of features and claim that simpler classifiers with profuse feature knowledge can outperform several complex machine-learning techniques in stance detection. Riedel et al. (2017) use a Multi Layer Perceptron (MLP) having a single hidden layer with term frequency and TF-IDF vectors as inputs to perform at par with several complex models. These works lend weight to our hypothesis that handcrafted and count-based features can significantly aid in the task of stance detection.

Recent work in stance classification shows extensive use of deep-learning models to achieve state-of-the-art results. Fajcik et al. (2019) and Yang et al. (2019) who worked on the same task and dataset as this work, use the BERT and GPT architectures respectively for stance classification. Fajcik et al. (2019) use an ensemble model wherein they combine outputs from several BERT models to increase the F1-score. Their system achieves a significantly high F1-score without the use of any hand-crafted features. Yang et al. (2019), who achieved state of the art results on this dataset prior to this work, use an inference chain based system that was fine-tuned on GPT. They use handcrafted features such as the presence of question marks, URLs, positive and negative words, etc. and leverage the structure of a conversation thread to achieve state-of-the-art results in stance classification.

### 2.1 Class-imbalance

Since most data sets based on real-world data (including the stance detection data set used in these experiments) suffer from class-imbalance, we explore recent methods of addressing this issue. One method of addressing class imbalance is the use of a two-step classifier, such as work by Wang et al. (2017). They first classify the tweets as 'comment' and 'non-comment' and use a second classifier to distinguish non-comments as 'Support', 'Deny', or 'Query'. Krawczyk et al. (2017), on the other hand, propose a one-vs-one decomposition of the multi-class problem before then combining the outputs of these binary classifiers using a weighted approach to rebuild the multi-class problem. Yang et al. (2019), on the other hand, use examples from similar data sets to increase the training data for minority classes.

The other method of handling class-imbalance is by use of cost-weighting. Tayyar Madabushi et al. (2019) apply cost-sensitive learning for the task of Fine-Grained Analysis of Propaganda in News Article (Da San Martino et al., 2019) wherein they first test the similarity between training and validation sets using Wilcoxon signed-rank test. They also show that cost-weighting (increasing the cost of a minority class) can be more beneficial when applied to dissimilar datasets. Fajcik et al. (2019) also use cost-weighting to tackle class-imbalance.

## 3 Experimental and Model Design

This section describes initial exploratory experiments and the process behind building a model that address the two obstacles to integrating features into pre-trained models mentioned in Section 1.1, namely: **a)** the significant difference in the number of epochs required by pre-trained models and feature based models, and **b**) the fact that using raw features might contain too much noise in an ensemble, the outputs alone might contain too little information, and dimensionality reduction methods result in the loss of task specific information.

### 3.1 Pre-Processing and Experimental Setup

The pre-processing steps used for all our experiments were consistent. URLs and mentions present in all the source and the reply posts were replaced with the special tokens '$URL$' and '$MENTION$' respectively. This was adapted from Fajcik et al. (2019) and found to be helpful in our experiments.

We use two sequences as input to pre-trained model, which represent an opinion (the $1^{st}$ sequence) and its target (the $2^{nd}$ sequence). It is the $1^{st}$ sequence, the opinion, that we are interested in classifying. This first sequence consists of the reply being classified and, in instances where such a post is itself a reply to another reply, is concatenated with its 'parent'. Figure 1 illustrates the tree structure of a conversation thread from the dataset.

Inputs to the pre-trained models were generated as follows: **(1)** While classifying the source post of a conversation thread (TE-1 in Figure 1), the text of this source post is the first input sequence (the one being classified). Since this post is not a reply and the target information is not explicitly available, the second input sequence is empty. **(2)** When classifying a reply (for example, TE-2 in Figure 1), the text of this reply is the first input sequence and the source post of the conversation thread becomes the second sequence. **(3)** While classifying a nested reply (reply to a reply, such as TE-3 in Figure 1), the text of this nested reply is concatenated with the text of its parent and used as the first input sequence, and the source post of the entire conversation thread becomes the second sequence. This method of structuring the input was adapted from work by Fajcik et al. (2019) who hypothesise that the stance of a given post depends on itself, its previous post and the source post of the conversation thread.

We use the *encode_plus* function provided by HuggingFace in their re-implementation of RoBERTa to encode the input sequences. The input sequences are first appended with special tokens - RoBERTa uses special tokens to indicate the start of the input ($< s >$), the end ($< /s >$) and two end tags to differentiate between different input sequences ($< /s >< /s >$). Figure 1 illustrates how special tokens were embedded in each example. These sequences are then encoded using Byte-Pair encoding and fed to RoBERTa.

### 3.2 Exploratory Experiments

Initial experiments using BERT yielded an F1-score of 0 for the class 'Deny', one of the harder to predict labels (See table 1). RoBERTa, however, produced an F1-score greater than 0 for all 4 classes, which led us to pick RoBERTa over BERT. We pre-process each example and feed two sequences as input to RoBERTa (as explained in section 3.1).

Next, we attempt to find a set of features that help in stance classification. As discussed in Section 1.1, work by Somasundaran and Wiebe (2010) on ideological stance classification showed that a unigram model can outperform more complex models. While their study was on a different problem set and focused on binary classification ('for' and 'against') of ideological stance, they showed that the stance of an opinion could be related to the kind of words used to express it. This is particularly true of a the 'Deny' class in the data set we work with. As discussed in section 1.1, words such as 'Not true' and 'Disagree' are frequently used to deny a claim.

We train a Multi Layer Perceptron (MLP) using TF-IDF features as input. We use a single hidden layer consisting of 128 hidden units, a tanh activation function and a final linear layer with a softmax function to make predictions. We use a learning rate of 0.02 and train this model for 55 epochs (Additional details such as the complete list of hyperparameter are available as part of the program code released). This model achieves an F1-score on 'Deny' class greater than that achieved using the RoBERTa-base (See table 1).

These results indicate that the use of TF-IDF features was particularly beneficial in classifying 'Deny'. In their recent work, Lim and Tayyar Madabushi (2020) incorporate TF-IDF features with BERT to improved performance on Offensive Language Identification in Social Media (Zampieri et al., 2020).

**Source Post (TE-1)**: Darren Wilson is a six year veteran of the #Ferguson Police and had no disciplinary actions against him. **[Support]**

  **Reply 1 (TE-2)**: Can we see video proof **[Query]**

  **Reply 2 (TE-3)**: HE ISN'T THE SHOOTER RT [MENTION] **[Comment]**

    **Reply 2.1 (TE-4)**: [MENTION] well who is #Ferguson **[Comment]**

---

**TE-1**: $< s >$ Darren Wilson is a six year veteran of the #Ferguson Police and had no disciplinary actions against him. $< /s > < /s > < /s >$

**TE-2**: $< s >$ Can we see video proof $< /s > < /s >$ Darren Wilson is a six year veteran of the #Ferguson Police and had no disciplinary actions against him. $< /s >$

**TE-3**: $< s >$ HE ISN'T THE SHOOTER RT [MENTION] $< /s > < /s >$ Darren Wilson is a six year veteran of the #Ferguson Police and had no disciplinary actions against him. $< /s >$

**TE-4**: $< s >$ [MENTION] well who is #Ferguson HE ISN'T THE SHOOTER RT [MENTION] $< /s > < /s >$ Darren Wilson is a six year veteran of the #Ferguson Police and had no disciplinary actions against him. $< /s >$

Figure 1: An example of a conversation thread and associated labels (in bold at the end of each post) from the RumourEval data set showing the tree like structure. The second part shows the training examples (TE) constructed for use in pre-trained models from each of the original posts. Further details in text.

This shows that tasks like stance classification and abuse detection greatly benefit from information pertaining to the words used in expressing that emotion.

| Model | Macro F1-Test | F1 Support | F1 Deny | F1 Query | F1 Comment |
|---|---|---|---|---|---|
| MLP Model | 0.38 | 0.18 | 0.24 | 0.22 | 0.87 |
| BERT | 0.46 | 0.44 | 0.0 | 0.52 | 0.90 |
| RoBERTa-base | 0.51 | 0.46 | 0.14 | 0.52 | 0.91 |
| RoBERTa-base + All TF-IDF Features | 0.49 | 0.45 | 0.06 | 0.53 | 0.91 |
| RoBERTa-base + PCA Transformed TF-IDF | 0.56 | 0.34 | 0.46 | 0.54 | 0.89 |
| RoBERTa-base + Output of MLP | 0.51 | 0.46 | 0.19 | 0.50 | 0.91 |

Table 1: Achieved results on the test set for Exploratory Models

Given the improved performance of the MLP on 'Deny', we aim to create an ensemble of the MLP and a pre-trained model so as to boost the overall performance. We ensemble the pooled output of RoBERTa with the output of a Multi-Layered Perceptron (MLP) (consisting of 4 units, one for each class). This combination is then connected to a linear layer followed by a softmax function to make predictions. While this model performed slightly better on the 'Deny' class, it performed worse on the class 'Query', thus achieving an overall Macro F1 score exactly equal to RoBERTa Base. We also create an ensemble model combining all the TF-IDF features with RoBERTa which we train for 4 epochs. This model performs worse than RoBERTa-base.

In order to verify that this decrease in performance is related to the TF-IDF features being high dimensional and noisy, we conduct experiments wherein we apply Principal Component Analysis (PCA), to reduce the dimensions of the TF-IDF vector to a length of 128 before using this shortened vector in the ensemble. We train this ensemble model for 40 epochs and note an increase in performance over the first 4 epochs and a subsequent increase in loss (with no change in accuracy) indicating that the model overfits. We similarly train the ensemble of RoBERTa and the MLP for 20 epochs and find that the model dramatically overfits with a drop in F1 from 0.51 to 0.15.

This section described experiments on six different models (See Table 1 for comparative results, we use the macro-averaged F1-score to compare models). Our finds are that **a)** the use of an MLP can be beneficial in boosting performance, **b)** the use of all tf-idf features in an ensemble is too noisy, **c)** the output of the MLP alone contains too little information to be useful in an ensemble, and **d)** ensembles of pre-trained models and an MLP will suffer from over-fitting before the MLP can be trained sufficiently. Additionally, training an ensemble of an MLP and RoBERTa takes about 10 min per epoch thus dramatically increasing the training time when we train for 20 or 40 epochs.

We address these shortcomings by introduction of a novel architecture that makes use of an *already trained MLP* which prevents overfitting, reduces train time while also ensuring the effective integration of pre-trained models and handcrafted features. The next Section (3.3) describes this model.

### 3.3 Model Architecture

This section describes the novel ensemble architecture that was used to incorporate count-based features, particularly useful for the classification of posts belonging to 'Deny', while simultaneously addressing the difficulties in ensembling feature based models and pre-trained models.

Figure 2 provides an illustration of the proposed architecture. This ensemble architecture uses two novel elements to address the two difficulties in creating an ensemble of the feature based and pre-trained models. Specifically **a)** the MLP used in the ensemble is one that *is already trained and optimised* (hyperparameters) for this task, and **b)** the output of the *hidden layer* of this already trained MLP is used in ensembling with pre-trained models instead of either the input or the final output.

The use of an already trained MLP in the ensemble ensures that the MLP does not underfit when trained in an ensemble with pre-trained models for a small number of epochs. This method, while similar to pre-training is not exactly the same as it is trained on the same task unlike in pre-training. The use of the hidden layer in the ensemble simultaneously deals with the problem of having too much noise in the input and too little information in the output by providing an abstract layer of condensed information from the MLP as input to the final ensemble model.

More concretely, this ensemble model is constructed as follows: The pooled output from RoBERTa (vector of length 768) is concatenated with the output of the hidden layer (vector of length 128) of an already trained MLP. This combined vector, having a length of 896, is further connect to a linear layer and a softmax function to make predictions (See Figure 2). We train this ensemble model for 6 epochs with a learning rate of $2e^{-6}$ and batch size 4. Further details on this model are available in the program code released as part of this work. We also test on ensembling the output of an already trained MLP instead of the hidden layer, and while it does do better than RoBERTa alone, it does not do as well as an ensemble of the hidden layer.

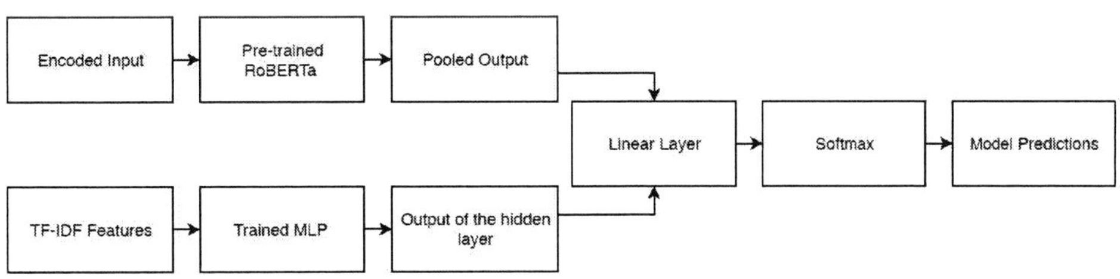


Figure 2: Architecture of the Proposed Model which combines output from RoBERTa and the hidden layer of an already trained MLP model.

This ensemble model outperforms RoBERTa along with all previously used ensemble models. We find this result, presented in Table 2, to be consistent across both RoBERTa-base and RoBERTa-large.

To address the possibility that our model was caught in local optima, we train each of our models 5 times using different seeds and evaluate them using the development set. We then use the model that performs the best on the development set to classify the test set and report results.

### 3.4 Tackling Class-imbalance

Class-imbalance implies that the number of training examples of one or more classes are significantly lower than the other classes. The RumourEval data set suffers from this same problem (Support 13.9%, Deny 6.6%, Query 4.8% and Comment 72.4%), and the 'Comment' class is not only dominant in the data set but is also the least helpful in detecting rumour (Gorrell et al., 2019). While there are several ways of handling class-imbalance (as discussed in section 2.1), we make use of cost-weighting due to its flexibility and proven performance.

Cost-weighting consists of assigning a higher weight to a minority class which holds more relevance. The cost function is thus modified to accommodate the weights assigned to each class - the more the weight, the more the model is penalised for inaccurate predictions on that class. The cost weights for our models were empirically determined via experiments and significantly boosted performance. We incorporate cost-weighting in all our experimented models.

## 4 Results and Analysis

This section presents an overview of our experiments and findings. We compare our results with prior state-of-the-art work on stance classification which makes use of this data set. We also perform an error analysis of our proposed model and report findings.

### 4.1 Results

Table 2 presents the macro-averaged F1-score we obtained by our proposed model (an ensemble model combining RoBERTa's pooled output with the output of the hidden layer of an already trained MLP). We also present results from both RoBERTa-base and RoBERTa-large to draw attention to how our proposed method significantly improves performance on both these versions of RoBERTa. For each experiment, we also report the macro-averaged F1-score and the F1-scores for all classes. These results show how how our proposed architecture significantly improves accuracy on the previously under-performing class 'Deny', which our count-based features were designed to improve.

| Model | Macro F1-Test | F1 Support | F1 Deny | F1 Query | F1 Comment |
|---|---|---|---|---|---|
| RoBERTa-base | 0.51 | 0.46 | 0.14 | 0.52 | 0.91 |
| RoBERTa-base + Hidden layer output of Trained MLP | **0.58** | **0.43** | **0.39** | **0.58** | **0.92** |
| RoBERTa-large | 0.57 | 0.43 | 0.42 | 0.54 | 0.92 |
| RoBERTa-large + Hidden layer output of Trained MLP **(Proposed Model)** | **0.64** | **0.48** | **0.55** | **0.60** | **0.93** |

Table 2: Results of our Proposed architecture on the test set using RoBERTa-base and RoBERTa-large showing a consistent improvement in performance across both versions of RoBERTa.

Table 3 presents our results alongside top performing systems on this dataset. We compare our results with the winning teams of SemEval 2019 for the same task. A branch-LSTM based system was used as a baseline for the stance classification task of SemEval 2019. We note that the model proposed in this work achieves state-of-the-art results on this dataset.

| System | Details | Macro Averaged F1-Score (%) |
|---|---|---|
| **This work** | | **63.94** |
| Yang et al. (2019) | 1st Rank - SemEval 2019 | 61.87 |
| Fajcik et al. (2019) | 2nd Rank - SemEval 2019 | 61.67 |
| Kochkina et al. (2017) | Baseline - SemEval 2019 (Winning method, SemEval 2017) | 49.3 |

Table 3: A comparison of this work with prior state-of-the-art methods on the same task and data set.

### 4.2 Discussion

Previous sections provided details of the various models we experimented with, along with their results on the test set. In this section we present an overview of our intuitions behind and observations from these experiments.

Our initial experiments showed how a feature based model can outperform pre-trained models *on specific classes*. This is a rather intuitive result which could potentially be true of various tasks that benefit from handcrafted and count-based features. We reiterate that tasks related to disinformation, propaganda and rumour are particularly capable of benefiting from handcrafted and count-based features such as user information, hashtags, URLs, word frequencies, and so on, as these features provide additional information that can be useful in classification and possibly unavailable to pre-trained models pre-trained on corpora that are different from social media and fine-tuned on the task over very few epochs.

We then presented two significant challenges (Section 3.2) that are faced in creating an ensemble of features and pre-trained models such as BERT or RoBERTa. We addressed the first challenge of too many or too few input features to be combined with pre-trained models by using the output of the MLP's hidden layer. We then address the second challenge - the difference in the number of training epochs required by feature-based and pre-trained models - by use of an already trained MLP.

The experiments with the ensemble model using RoBERTa's pooled output and the output of the trained MLP model showed a significant increase in model performance on stance classification. We show how we address each challenge through our experiments and propose a novel architecture that utilises abstract information from a trained MLP to increase the performance of pre-trained models.

In summary, this work shows that stance classification systems benefit from features that depict the kind of words used to express an opinion by ensembling TF-IDF features with RoBERTa. We also propose a novel architecture to effectively integrate a feature engineered model with pre-trained deep learning models so as to significantly boost performance on tasks that benefit from handcrafted features (such as stance classification).

### 4.3 Error Analysis

We perform an extensive error analysis of our proposed model. First, we study the impact of availability of trained features to RoBERTa for stance classification. As depicted from the confusion matrix (Table 4), the ensemble model using the abstract features from the trained MLP model specifically improves the performance of 'Support', 'Deny' and 'Query' classes. Our model performs exceedingly well on the 'Deny' class, which previous models have typically struggled with. However, this comes at the cost of misclassifying some other classes ('Support' and 'Comment') as 'Deny', it increases the overall F1-score. This observation is detailed further using examples from the data set.

An analysis of the predictions made by the model on the test set shows that it learns to associate words such as 'Fake', 'not' and 'not true' with the 'Deny' class. Again, this shows that effective integration of features by use of trained MLP models can significantly help in the classification of output classes that benefit from such features. While this was helpful in the classification of most examples from the 'Deny' class, some posts that used the aforementioned words were 'comments' and misclassified as 'Deny' (Refer Note 1 from Table 5). Similarly, some 'comments' that contained interrogative words

| True label | Predicted label | | | |
|---|---|---|---|---|
| | Support | Deny | Query | Comment |
| Support | **53 (46)** | 4 (1) | 1 (1) | 99 (109) |
| Deny | 1 (1) | **52 (31)** | 3 (2) | 45 (67) |
| Query | 14 (11) | 6 (4) | **52 (47)** | 21 (31) |
| Comment | 1 (1) | 26 (12) | 22 (31) | **1427 (1432)** |

Table 4: Confusion matrix for RoBERTa-large and RoBERTa-large + Trained MLP models. Values associated with RoBERTa-large are in brackets.

and question marks were classified as 'Queries' without taking the content of the post into consideration (Refer Note 2 from table 5). This is interesting as it reintroduces the problems encountered by earlier models - problems that were, to some extent, addressed by contextual pre-trained models, showing the need for a careful balance between these two approaches.

| Note | Reply-post | Target | Predicted label | True label |
|---|---|---|---|---|
| 1 | *$MENTION$ If this is fake, the poster should be charged with spreading mass panic* | *This is crazy! #CapeTown #capestorm #weather-forecast $URL$* | Deny | Comment |
| 2 | *Why would I need a kettle?* | *Is it true most Americans don't own a kettle? If so, why not?* | Query | Comment |

Table 5: Error Analysis of predictions by the RoBERTa + trained MLP ensemble model on the test data. While the model learns to associate words like 'Fake' and 'why' with the 'Deny' and 'Query' classes respectively, it gives too much weight to these features, resulting in errors.

The model also finds it challenging to distinguish between a 'support' and a 'comment' with respect to a post - a problem that could be attributed these two classes being somewhat similar. The model is also not able to classify posts that contain a URL, possible due to the missing information from the URL. Finally, the model also often inaccurately predicts the labels of the source post. We believe that this is due to the explicit unavailability of target information.

## 5 Conclusions and Future Work

This work introduced a novel architecture that makes use of abstract information from an already trained MLP to boost RoBERTa on the task of stance detection. Our technique achieves state-of-the-art results with an accuracy of 86.69% and a macro-averaged F1-score of 63.94 on a standard data set. We conclude that an effective integration of features with models such as RoBERTa can significantly increase model performance on tasks that benefit from such features and that our architecture is an effective solution.

In future work we aim to integrate entire conversational threads to study its impact of such information as, in this work, we limit the information pertaining to one example to reply, previous and the source post of the conversation thread. We also aim to use these methods on other related propaganda and abuse datasets along with exploring the impact of other handcrafted features.

## Acknowledgements

We would like to thank the NVIDIA Deep Learning Institute for the provision of AWS credits which we used to access GPU resources in this work.

## References


A. Aker, Leon Derczynski, and Kalina Bontcheva. 2017. Simple open stance classification for rumour analysis. In *RANLP*.

Hareesh Bahuleyan and Olga Vechtomova. 2017. UWaterloo at SemEval-2017 task 8: Detecting stance towards rumours with topic independent features. In *Proceedings of the 11th International Workshop on Semantic Evaluation (SemEval-2017)*, pages 461–464, Vancouver, Canada, August. Association for Computational Linguistics.

Giovanni Da San Martino, Seunghak Yu, Alberto Barrón-Cedeño, Rostislav Petrov, and Preslav Nakov. 2019. Fine-grained analysis of propaganda in news article. In *Proceedings of the 2019 Conference on Empirical Methods in Natural Language Processing and the 9th International Joint Conference on Natural Language Processing (EMNLP-IJCNLP)*, pages 5636–5646, Hong Kong, China, November. Association for Computational Linguistics.

Leon Derczynski, Kalina Bontcheva, Michal Lukasik, Thierry Declerck, Arno Scharl, Georgi Georgiev, Petya Osenova, Toms Pariente Lobo, Anna Kolliakou, Robert Stewart, et al. 2015. Pheme: Computing veracity—the fourth challenge of big social data. In *Proceedings of the Extended Semantic Web Conference EU Project Networking session (ESCW-PN)*.

Jacob Devlin, Ming-Wei Chang, Kenton Lee, and Kristina Toutanova. 2019. BERT: Pre-training of deep bidirectional transformers for language understanding. In *Proceedings of the 2019 Conference of the North American Chapter of the Association for Computational Linguistics: Human Language Technologies, Volume 1 (Long and Short Papers)*, pages 4171–4186, Minneapolis, Minnesota, June. Association for Computational Linguistics.

Joan Donovon. 2020. Covid hoaxes are using a loophole to stay alive—even after content is deleted. *MIT Technology Review*.

Martin Fajcik, Pavel Smrz, and Lukas Burget. 2019. BUT-FIT at SemEval-2019 task 7: Determining the rumour stance with pre-trained deep bidirectional transformers. In *Proceedings of the 13th International Workshop on Semantic Evaluation*, pages 1097–1104, Minneapolis, Minnesota, USA, June. Association for Computational Linguistics.

Genevieve Gorrell, Elena Kochkina, Maria Liakata, Ahmet Aker, Arkaitz Zubiaga, Kalina Bontcheva, and Leon Derczynski. 2019. SemEval-2019 task 7: RumourEval, determining rumour veracity and support for rumours. In *Proceedings of the 13th International Workshop on Semantic Evaluation*, pages 845–854, Minneapolis, Minnesota, USA, June. Association for Computational Linguistics.

Kazi Saidul Hasan and Vincent Ng. 2013. Stance classification of ideological debates: Data, models, features, and constraints. In *Proceedings of the Sixth International Joint Conference on Natural Language Processing*, pages 1348–1356, Nagoya, Japan, October. Asian Federation of Natural Language Processing.

Y. Linlin Huang, Kate Starbird, Mania Orand, Stephanie A. Stanek, and Heather T. Pedersen. 2015. Connected through crisis: Emotional proximity and the spread of misinformation online. In *Proceedings of the 18th ACM Conference on Computer Supported Cooperative Work & Social Computing*, CSCW '15, page 969–980, New York, NY, USA. Association for Computing Machinery

Soo-Min Kim and Eduard Hovy. 2007. Crystal: Analyzing predictive opinions on the web. In *Proceedings of the 2007 Joint Conference on Empirical Methods in Natural Language Processing and Computational Natural Language Learning (EMNLP-CoNLL)*, pages 1056–1064, Prague, Czech Republic, June. Association for Computational Linguistics.

Elena Kochkina, Maria Liakata, and Isabelle Augenstein. 2017. Turing at SemEval-2017 task 8: Sequential approach to rumour stance classification with branch-LSTM. In *Proceedings of the 11th International Workshop on Semantic Evaluation (SemEval-2017)*, pages 475–480, Vancouver, Canada, August. Association for Computational Linguistics.

Bartosz Krawczyk, Bridget T McInnes, and Alberto Cano. 2017. Sentiment classification from multi-class imbalanced twitter data using binarization. In *International Conference on Hybrid Artificial Intelligence Systems*, pages 26–37. Springer.

Wah Meng Lim and Harish Tayyar Madabushi. 2020. Uob at semeval-2020 task 12: Boosting bert with corpus level information. *ArXiv*, abs/2008.08547.

Wei-Hao Lin, Theresa Wilson, Janyce Wiebe, and Alexander Hauptmann. 2006. Which side are you on? identifying perspectives at the document and sentence levels. In *Proceedings of the Tenth Conference on Computational Natural Language Learning (CoNLL-X)*, pages 109–116, New York City, June. Association for Computational Linguistics.

Y. Liu, Myle Ott, Naman Goyal, Jingfei Du, Mandar Joshi, Danqi Chen, Omer Levy, M. Lewis, Luke Zettlemoyer, and Veselin Stoyanov. 2019. Roberta: A robustly optimized bert pretraining approach. *ArXiv*, abs/1907.11692.

Alec Radford, Karthik Narasimhan, Tim Salimans, and Ilya Sutskever. 2018. Improving language understanding by generative pre-training.

Benjamin Riedel, Isabelle Augenstein, Georgios P Spithourakis, and Sebastian Riedel. 2017. A simple but tough-to-beat baseline for the fake news challenge stance detection task. *arXiv preprint arXiv:1707.03264*.

Swapna Somasundaran and Janyce Wiebe. 2010. Recognizing stances in ideological on-line debates. In *Proceedings of the NAACL HLT 2010 Workshop on Computational Approaches to Analysis and Generation of Emotion in Text*, CAAGET '10, page 116–124, USA. Association for Computational Linguistics.

Harish Tayyar Madabushi, Elena Kochkina, and Michael Castelle. 2019. Cost-sensitive BERT for generalisable sentence classification on imbalanced data. In *Proceedings of the Second Workshop on Natural Language Processing for Internet Freedom: Censorship, Disinformation, and Propaganda*, pages 125–134, Hong Kong, China, November. Association for Computational Linguistics.

Feixiang Wang, Man Lan, and Yuanbin Wu. 2017. ECNU at SemEval-2017 task 8: Rumour evaluation using effective features and supervised ensemble models. In *Proceedings of the 11th International Workshop on Semantic Evaluation (SemEval-2017)*, pages 491–496, Vancouver, Canada, August. Association for Computational Linguistics.

Ruoyao Yang, Wanying Xie, Chunhua Liu, and Dong Yu. 2019. BLCU_NLP at SemEval-2019 task 7: An inference chain-based GPT model for rumour evaluation. In *Proceedings of the 13th International Workshop on Semantic Evaluation*, pages 1090–1096, Minneapolis, Minnesota, USA, June. Association for Computational Linguistics.

Marcos Zampieri, Preslav Nakov, Sara Rosenthal, Pepa Atanasova, Georgi Karadzhov, Hamdy Mubarak, Leon Derczynski, Zeses Pitenis, and Çağrı Çöltekin. 2020. Semeval-2020 task 12: Multilingual offensive language identification in social media (offenseval 2020).

A. Zubiaga, A. Aker, Kalina Bontcheva, Maria Liakata, and R. Procter. 2018. Detection and resolution of rumours in social media. *ACM Computing Surveys (CSUR)*, 51:1 – 36.

# A Multi-Modal Method for Satire Detection using Textual and Visual Cues

**Lily Li[1], Or Levi[2], Pedram Hosseini[3], David A. Broniatowski[3]**
[1]Jericho Senior High School, New York, USA
[2]AdVerifai, Amsterdam, Netherlands
[3]The George Washington University, Washington D.C., USA
lily.li@jerichoapps.org, or@adverifai.com
{phosseini,broniatowski}@gwu.edu

## Abstract

Satire is a form of humorous critique, but it is sometimes misinterpreted by readers as legitimate news, which can lead to harmful consequences. We observe that the images used in satirical news articles often contain absurd or ridiculous content and that image manipulation is used to create fictional scenarios. While previous work have studied text-based methods, in this work we propose a multi-modal approach based on state-of-the-art visiolinguistic model ViLBERT. To this end, we create a new dataset consisting of images and headlines of regular and satirical news for the task of satire detection. We fine-tune ViLBERT on the dataset and train a convolutional neural network that uses an image forensics technique. Evaluation on the dataset shows that our proposed multi-modal approach outperforms image-only, text-only, and simple fusion baselines.

## 1 Introduction

Satire is a literary device that writers employ to mock or ridicule a person, group, or ideology by passing judgment on them for a cultural transgression or poor social behavior. Satirical news utilizes humor and irony by placing the target of the criticism into a ridiculous, fictional situation that the reader must suspend their disbelief and go along with (Maslo, 2019). However, despite what absurd content satirical news may contain, it is often mistaken by readers as real, legitimate news, which may then lead to the unintentional spread of misinformation. In a recent survey conducted by The Conversation (Garrett et al., 2019), up to 28% of Republican respondents and 14% of Democratic respondents reported that they believed stories fabricated by the Babylon Bee, a satirical news website, to be "definitely true". In these instances, the consequences of satire are indistinguishable from those of fake news.

To reduce the spread of misinformation, social media platforms have partnered with third-party fact-checkers to flag false news articles and tag articles from known satirical websites as satire for users (Facebook, nd; Google, nd). However, due to the high cost and relative inefficiency of employing experts to manually annotate articles, many researchers have tackled the challenge of automated satire detection. Existing models for satirical news detection have yet to explore the visual domain of satire, even though image thumbnails of news articles may convey information that reveals or disproves the satirical nature of the articles. In the field of cognitive-linguistics, Maslo (2019) observed the use of altered images showing imaginary scenarios on the satirical news show The Daily Show. This phenomenon also extends to satirical news articles, as seen in Figure 1. For example, Figure 1(A) depicts the Marvel Cinematic Universe character Hulk from the film Avengers: Infinity War and the United States President Donald Trump spliced together. Alone, each of the two images is serious and not satirical, but, since they come from drastically different contexts, combining the two images creates a clearly ridiculous thumbnail that complements the headline of the article.

In our work, we propose a multi-modal method for detecting satirical news articles. We hypothesize that 1) the content of news thumbnail images when combined with text, and 2) detecting the presence of manipulated or added characters and objects, can aid in the identification of satirical articles.





*Proceedings of the 3rd NLP4IF Workshop on NLP for Internet Freedom*, pages 33–38
Barcelona, Spain (Online), December 12, 2020

Figure 1: Examples of satirical news images created by altering existing images.

## 2 Related Work

Previous work proposed methods for satirical news detection using textual content (Levi et al., 2019). Some works utilize classical machine learning algorithms such as SVM with handcrafted features from factual and satirical news headlines and body text, including bag-of-words, n-grams, and lexical features (Burfoot and Baldwin, 2009; Rubin et al., 2016). More recent works use deep learning to extract learned features for satire detection. Yang et al. (2017) proposed a hierarchical model with attention mechanism and handcrafted linguistic features to understand satire at a paragraph and article-level.

While previous work utilize visiolinguistic data for similar tasks, there is no related work that employs multi-modal data to classify articles into satirical and factual news. Nakamura et al. (2019) created a dataset containing images and text for fake news detection in posts on the social media website Reddit. While they include a category for satire/parody in their 6-way dataset, since they use only content that has been submitted by Reddit users, it is not representative of mainstream news media. Multi-modal approaches have also been tried in sarcasm detection; Castro et al. (2019) compiled a dataset of scenes from popular TV shows and Cai et al. (2019) used tweets comprising of text and images from Twitter.

## 3 Methods

### 3.1 Data

We create a new multi-modal dataset of satirical and regular news articles. The satirical news is collected from four websites that explicitly declare themselves to be satire, and the regular news is collected from six mainstream news websites[1]. Specifically, the satirical news websites we collect articles from are The Babylon Bee, Clickhole, Waterford Whisper News, and The DailyER. The regular news websites are Reuters, The Hill, Politico, New York Post, Huffington Post, and Vice News. We collect the headlines and the thumbnail images of the latest 1000 articles for each of the publications. The dataset contains a total of 4000 satirical and 6000 regular news articles.

### 3.2 Proposed Models

**Multi-Modal Learning.** We use Vision & Language BERT (ViLBERT), a multi-modal model proposed by Lu et al. (2019) that processes images and text in two separate streams. Each stream consists of

[1] The regular news websites we use are listed by Media Bias/Fact Check `https://mediabiasfactcheck.com/`, a volunteer-run and nonpartisan organization dedicated to fact-checking and determining the bias of news publications

transformer blocks based on BERT (Devlin et al., 2018) and co-attentive layers that facilitate interaction between the visual and textual modalities. In each co-attentive transformer layer, multi-head attention is computed the same as a standard transformer block except the visual modality attends to the textual modality and vice-versa. To learn representations for vision-and-language tasks, ViLBERT is pre-trained using the masked multi-model modeling and multi-modal alignment prediction tasks on the Conceptual Captions dataset (Sharma et al., 2018). We choose to use ViLBERT because of its high performance on a variety of visiolinguistic tasks, including Visual Question Answering, Image Retrieval, and Visual Commonsense Reasoning. We fine-tune ViLBERT on the satire detection dataset by passing the element-wise product of the final image and text representations into a learned classification layer.

**Image Forgery Detection.** Since satirical news images are often forged from two or more images (known as image splicing), we implement an additional model that uses error level analysis (ELA). ELA is an image forensics technique that takes advantage of lossy JPEG compression for image tampering detection (Krawetz, 2007). In ELA, each JPEG image is resaved at a known compression rate, and the absolute pixel-by-pixel differences between the original and the resaved images are compared. ELA can be used to identify image manipulations where a lower quality image was spliced into a higher quality image or vice-versa. To detect image forgeries as an indicator of satirical news, we preprocess the images using ELA with a compression rate of 90% and use them as input into a CNN.

For the CNN, we use two convolutional layers with 32 kernels and a filter width of 5, each followed by a max-pooling layer. The output features from the CNN are fed into a MLP with a hidden size of 256 and a classification layer. We pretrain the model on the CASIA 2.0 image tampering detection dataset (Dong et al., 2013) before fine-tuning on the images of the satire detection dataset.

**Implemention.** We divide the data into training and test sets with a ratio of 80%:20%. We train all our models with a batch size of 32 and Adam optimizer. We use the MMF (Singh et al., 2020) implementation of ViLBERT and fine-tune it for 12 epochs with a learning rate of 5e-6. We extract Mask RCNN (He et al., 2017) features from the images in the dataset as visual input. The ViLBERT model has 6 transformer blocks in the visual stream and 12 transformer blocks in the textual stream. Our ELA+CNN model is trained with a learning rate of 1e-5 for 7 epochs.[2]

### 3.3 Baselines

To create fair baselines for our fine-tuned ViLBERT model, we train multi-modal models that use simple fusion. In the model denoted as Concatenation, ResNet-101 (He et al., 2016) and BERT features are concatenated and a MLP is trained on top. In the model denoted as Average fusion, the output of ResNet-101 and BERT are averaged. We choose these two models as our baselines to evaluate the effects of ViLBERT's early fusion of visual and textual representations and multi-modal pre-training on Conceptual Captions (Sharma et al., 2018). We also fine-tune uni-modal ResNet-101 and $\text{BERT}_{\text{BASE}}$ models to compare the performance of the multi-modal models to.

| Type | Model | Accuracy | F1 score | AUC-ROC |
|---|---|---|---|---|
| | All regular news | 60.00 | — | 50.00 |
| Baselines | ResNet101 | 73.54 | 65.26 | 80.28 |
| | $\text{BERT}_{\text{BASE}}$ | 91.33 | 88.64 | 96.77 |
| | Simple fusion (average) | 92.53 | 90.44 | 96.74 |
| | Simple fusion (concatenation) | 92.74 | 90.70 | 97.31 |
| Proposed Models | ELA+CNN | 44.20 | 51.86 | 44.61 |
| | ViLBERT | **93.80** | **92.16** | **98.03** |

Table 1: Model performance on satire detection dataset.

[2]Scripts for our experiments are available at: `https://github.com/lilyli2004/satire`

## 4 Results and Discussion

### 4.1 Experimental Results

We measure the performance of the proposed and baseline models using Accuracy, F1 score, and AUC-ROC metrics. The results are shown in Table 1. The models using only the visual modality (ResNet-101 and CNN+ELA) do not perform as well as the model that uses only the text modality ($\text{BERT}_{\text{BASE}}$). The simple fusion models (Average fusion, Concatenation) perform marginally better than $\text{BERT}_{\text{BASE}}$. ViLBERT outperforms the simple fusion multi-modal models because it uses early, deep fusion and has undergone multi-modal pre-training rather than only separate uni-modal visual and text pre-training. ViLBERT also performs almost 3.5 F1 points above the uni-modal $\text{BERT}_{\text{BASE}}$ model.

Surprisingly, the performance of the ELA+CNN model was very poor, achieving an accuracy worse than random chance. While this is not in line with our initial hypothesis, there might be several reasons for these results: Firstly, ELA is not able to detect image manipulations if the images have been resaved multiple times since after they have been compressed at a high rate there is little visible change in error levels (Krawetz, 2007). This makes it especially difficult to identify manipulation in images taken from the Internet, as they have usually undergone multiple resaves and are not camera originals. Additionally, although ELA can be used as a method to detect and localize the region of an image that has been potentially altered, it does not allow for the identification of what kind of image manipulation technique was used. This is important because even reputable news publications, such as Reuters and The Associated Press use Photoshop and other software to perform minor adjustments to photos, for example, to alter the coloring or lighting, or to blur the background (Schlesinger, 2007; The Associated Press, 2014).

Figure 2 shows examples from the satire detection dataset that illustrate the inconsistency of error level analysis in highlighting image manipulations. Both Figure 2(A) and Figure 2(B) are thumbnails from satirical articles that have clearly been fabricated. However, it is clear from the difference in ELA values that Figure 2(A) is a composite, while the ELA of Figure 2(B) is relatively uniform so the splicing can go undetected. Similarly, Figure 2(C) and Figure 2(D) are both thumbnails from factual articles, yet the drastic difference in ELA values of the building in Figure 2(C) indicates that it has undergone heavy editing while the ELA in Figure 2(D) does not.

Figure 2: Examples of images in the satire detection dataset and their ELA.

### 4.2 Model Misclassification Study

After classification, we randomly select 20% of the test set samples misclassified by ViLBERT and observed them for patterns across multiple samples. Figure 3 shows examples of misclassified samples. We observed three main reasons that may have been the cause of the incorrectly classified articles: The model misinterpreted the headline (Figure 3(A)), the model lacks knowledge of current events (Figure 3(B)), and the article covered a bizarre but true story (Figure 3(C)).

Figure 3(A) shows an article from Politico that has been classified as satire. The image does not portray anything strange or out of the ordinary. However, the headline uses the word "bursts", which the model might be incorrectly interpreting in the literal sense even though it is being used metaphorically.

If "bursts" was intended to be literal, it would drastically change the meaning of the text, which may be why the model failed to classify the article as factual. Figure 3(B) shows a satirical article from Babylon Bee that has been misclassified as factual. Its image has also not been heavily altered or faked; in fact, it is the same image that was used as the original thumbnail of the Joe Rogan podcast episode that is the subject of the article. However, the model fails to recognize the ridiculousness of the text, since it does not have the political knowledge to spot the contrast between the "alt-right" and the American politician Bernie Sanders. In Figure 3(C), an article is from the factual publication The New York Post is misclassified as satirical. Although both the headline and the image seem very ridiculous, the story and the image were, in fact, not fabricated. Thus, identifying text/images as absurd might not always aid in satire detection, since ViLBERT fails in classifying this article as factual because it is unable to tell that the image has not been forged.

Tammy Duckworth bursts into VP contention

Bernie Sanders Welcomed As Newest Member Of Alt-Right After Joe Rogan Endorsement

Cutout of Jeffrey Epstein appears in stands at UK soccer game

Figure 3: Examples of articles misclassified by ViLBERT

## 5 Conclusion and Future Investigations

In this paper, we create a multi-modal satire detection dataset and propose two models for the task based on the characteristics of satirical images and their relationships with the headlines. While our model based on image tampering detection performed significantly worse than the baselines, empirical evaluation showed the efficacy of our proposed multi-modal approach compared to simple fusion and uni-modal models. In future work on satire detection, we will incorporate image forensics methods to identify image splicing in satirical images, body text of articles instead of just headlines, as well as knowledge about politics and other current issues.

## References

Clint Burfoot and Timothy Baldwin. 2009. Automatic satire detection: Are you having a laugh? In *Proceedings of the ACL-IJCNLP 2009 Conference Short Papers*, pages 161–164, Suntec, Singapore, August. Association for Computational Linguistics.

Yitao Cai, Huiyu Cai, and Xiaojun Wan. 2019. Multi-modal sarcasm detection in twitter with hierarchical fusion model. In *Proceedings of the 57th Annual Meeting of the Association for Computational Linguistics*, pages 2506–2515, Florence, Italy, July. Association for Computational Linguistics.

Santiago Castro, Devamanyu Hazarika, Verónica Pérez-Rosas, Roger Zimmermann, Rada Mihalcea, and Soujanya Poria. 2019. Towards multimodal sarcasm detection (an _Obviously_ perfect paper). In *Proceedings of the 57th Annual Meeting of the Association for Computational Linguistics*, pages 4619–4629, Florence, Italy, July. Association for Computational Linguistics.

Jacob Devlin, Ming-Wei Chang, Kenton Lee, and Kristina Toutanova. 2018. BERT: Pre-training of deep bidirectional transformers for language understanding.

Jing Dong, Wei Wang, and Tieniu Tan. 2013. CASIA image tampering detection evaluation database. In *2013 IEEE China Summit and International Conference on Signal and Information Processing*, pages 422–426. IEEE.

Facebook. n.d. *Fact-checking on Facebook: What publishers should know*. Business Help Center.

R. Kelly Garrett, Robert Bond, and Shannon Poulsen, 2019. *Too many people think satirical news is real.*

Google. n.d. *What does each label mean?* Publisher Help Center.

Kaiming He, Xiangyu Zhang, Shaoqing Ren, and Jian Sun. 2016. Deep residual learning for image recognition. In *Proceedings of the IEEE conference on computer vision and pattern recognition*, pages 770–778.

Kaiming He, Georgia Gkioxari, Piotr Dollar, and Ross Girshick. 2017. Mask r-cnn. *2017 IEEE International Conference on Computer Vision (ICCV)*, Oct.

Neal Krawetz. 2007. A picture's worth: Digital image analysis and forensics. *Black Hat Briefings.*

Or Levi, Pedram Hosseini, Mona Diab, and David A. Broniatowski. 2019. Identifying nuances in fake news vs. satire: Using semantic and linguistic cues. *arXiv preprint arXiv:1910.01160.*

Jiasen Lu, Dhruv Batra, Devi Parikh, and Stefan Lee. 2019. Vilbert: Pretraining task-agnostic visiolinguistic representations for vision-and-language tasks. In *Advances in Neural Information Processing Systems*, pages 13–23.

Adi Maslo. 2019. Parsing satirical humor: a model of cognitive-linguistic satire analysis. *Književni jezik*, (30):231–253.

Kai Nakamura, Sharon Levy, and William Yang Wang. 2019. r/fakeddit: A new multimodal benchmark dataset for fine-grained fake news detection.

Victoria Rubin, Niall Conroy, Yimin Chen, and Sarah Cornwell. 2016. Fake news or truth? using satirical cues to detect potentially misleading news. In *Proceedings of the Second Workshop on Computational Approaches to Deception Detection*, pages 7–17, San Diego, California, June. Association for Computational Linguistics.

David Schlesinger. 2007. *The use of Photoshop.* Reuters Blogs Dashboard.

Piyush Sharma, Nan Ding, Sebastian Goodman, and Radu Soricut. 2018. Conceptual Captions: A cleaned, hypernymed, image alt-text dataset for automatic image captioning. In *Proceedings of the 56th Annual Meeting of the Association for Computational Linguistics (Volume 1: Long Papers)*, pages 2556–2565, Melbourne, Australia, July. Association for Computational Linguistics.

Amanpreet Singh, Vedanuj Goswami, Vivek Natarajan, Yu Jiang, Xinlei Chen, Meet Shah, Marcus Rohrbach, Dhruv Batra, and Devi Parikh. 2020. Mmf: A multimodal framework for vision and language research. `https://github.com/facebookresearch/mmf`.

The Associated Press. 2014. *AP News Values and Principals.*

Fan Yang, Arjun Mukherjee, and Eduard Dragut. 2017. Satirical news detection and analysis using attention mechanism and linguistic features. In *Proceedings of the 2017 Conference on Empirical Methods in Natural Language Processing*, pages 1979–1989, Copenhagen, Denmark, September. Association for Computational Linguistics.

# A Risk Communication Event Detection Model via Contrastive Learning

**Mingi Shin**[1], **Sungwon Han**[1], **Sungkyu Park**[2] and **Meeyoung Cha**[2,1]
[1] Korea Advanced Institute of Science and Technology (KAIST)
[2] Institute for Basic Science (IBS)
Daejeon, South Korea
{mingi.shin, lion4151, shaun.park, meeyoungcha}@kaist.ac.kr

## Abstract

This paper presents a time-topic cohesive model describing the communication patterns on the coronavirus pandemic from three Asian countries. The strength of our model is two-fold. First, it detects contextualized events based on topical and temporal information via contrastive learning. Second, it can be applied to multiple languages, enabling a comparison of risk communication across cultures. We present a case study and discuss future implications of the proposed model.

## 1 Introduction

The novel coronavirus disease (COVID-19) is affecting public health and the economy worldwide. The surge in social media usage during the pandemic led the online content to an excellent tool to examine risk communication (Lazer et al., 2018; Beaunoyer et al., 2020). As more people seek and share information online, NGOs and especially the WHO have warned of the danger of the increasing misinformation on the pandemic. A new term, *infodemic*, was coined to describe this phenomenon.

On the other hand, the natural language processing (NLP) community's recent developments enable in-depth analysis of topical changes from online resources. Latent Dirichlet Allocation (LDA) can detect major topics from unstructured text data (e.g., extract topics in the context of a global pandemic (Park et al., 2020)). Advanced language models like BERT can be used to learn representations (e.g., the pandemic discourse on Twitter (Müller et al., 2020)). A language-agnostic version of BERT further extends its capability to handle multiple languages (Gencoglu, 2020).

Despite social media's potential to understand the risk communication pattern and infodemic during the pandemic, several challenges remain. One of them is the temporal aspect. The existing topic models which exclude temporal information cannot represent how the conversations/themes developed over time (Blei and Lafferty, 2006). While some works propose the refinements of such models by incorporating the time or metadata information (Blei and Lafferty, 2006; Roberts et al., 2013), they still need to dissect the data into arbitrarily chosen time chunks. Particularly in risk communication, where the public attention evolves quickly in a short period, the contextual information intertwining topic and time becomes a critical component (Atefeh and Khreich, 2015). Considering the time aspect also allows identifying topics that are of significant influence yet over a short span of time.

Addressing the limitation above, we present a time-topic cohesive model to detect contextualized events and topics over time. Our model marries key ideas from contrastive learning (hereafter CL) and multilingual BERT (hereafter mBERT). CL is a machine learning and computer vision technique to classify similar objects by devising a triplet loss function among one anchor and two targets (Dai and Lin, 2017). By designing a triplet loss such as computing the difference of topic and time between anchor and target tweets, our model can jointly consider temporal and topical characteristics when detecting major events about the pandemic. mBERT allows us to apply the model to multiple countries for comparison.

The final model is applied to a collection of Twitter messages gathered from three Asian countries: South Korea, Vietnam, and Iran. Based on the determined events, we can understand what information (or misinformation) was mainly talked about at what stage of the pandemic in each country. Unlike





*Proceedings of the 3rd NLP4IF Workshop on NLP for Internet Freedom*, pages 39–43
Barcelona, Spain (Online), December 12, 2020

existing topic models, this new method also captures the temporal coherence of topics. We present a case study that shows how the risk communication on COVID-19 starts with several key events initially and then expands to diverse domains in South Korea.

## 2 Method

### 2.1 Data

We analyze GeoCoV19 (Qazi et al., 2020), a multilingual dataset of tweets about COVID-19 with location information. The data comprise tweets that contain COVID-19-related keywords in multiple languages. The coverage of data is for 90 days, from February 1 to May 1, 2020. We only utilize tweets written in Korean, Farsi, and Vietnamese, all local languages corresponding to South Korea, Iran, and Vietnam. This was done by constraining the language to the `lang` attribute, the auto-detected language of the tweet text. The total number of tweets were 43,347 (% of retweets: 79), 19,174 (34), and 4,359 (16) for each language.

The studied Asian countries had different epidemic situations. South Korea was one of the first countries affected by the virus, recording a surge in the increase of confirmed cases in February and March. By May, the country saw a flattening trend in the confirmed cases. Meanwhile, Iran is one of the most severely affected countries. Within our target period, the number of confirmed cases rapidly increased and maintained over several hundreds of cases. On the other hand, in Vietnam, the numbers have consistently stayed below a hundred throughout the data period.

**Preprocessing Data.** We excluded retweets, URLs, language-dependent stopwords, and redundant whitespace. We also replaced the mentioned names with a `UNK` token prior to analysis.

**LDA Topic Modeling.** We utilized the LDA model to extract topical information from the text. We first tokenized the tweet text by standard Python libraries for each specific language. We then trained the LDA model for 50 topics. Each tweet was labeled with the most probable topic.

### 2.2 Contextualized Event Detection over Time

We propose an event detection algorithm that considers word occurrence patterns and time concurrently. We regard tweets with similar word patterns but large time discrepancy as entries from different events. This approach for training is inspired by the CL approach. By constructing triplets that reflect the time and topical distance among tweets, optimizing triplet loss can directly lead the embedding to gather similar events within a short period. We then perform a clustering algorithm over the trained embeddings to extract the topic clusters. The structure of mBERT is utilized, and its pre-trained weights are used as initialization to distill contextualized information during training the embeddings.

Our model adds a linear layer on the concatenation of the pooled output from mBERT and the normalized timestamp (min-max scaling) to embed tweets within the fixed sized vector. Then, we project the concatenated vector into L2-normalized space. As a pooling strategy, we used the output from the `CLS`-token which is trained for the next sentence prediction. The result model is mBERT which has a spherical embedding head on the top. To fine-tune this model, we construct two kinds of triplets: (1) *LDA-dependent triplet*, in which anchor and positive tweets shows the same topic from the trained LDA model while negative does not; (2) *time-dependent triplet*, in which timestamp from positive tweet is nearer to the anchor than negative. We used a combined loss between the two triplet losses as an objective function. Given $a$ as an anchor Tweet, $p$ as a positive sample from the dataset and $n$ as a negative, two kinds of triplet loss ($L_{tri}$) can be defined below:

$$L_{tri\_topic} = \max\{s(w_a, w_n) - s(w_a, w_p) + \tau_{topic}, 0\} \tag{1}$$

$$L_{tri\_time} = \max\{s(w_a, w_n) - s(w_a, w_p) + \tau_{time}, 0\} \tag{2}$$

where $s$ is a similarity function, $\tau_{topic}$ and $\tau_{time}$ are thresholds, and $w_a, w_p, w_n$ are the embeddings from the model using $a, p, n$ as an input respectively. Since our embedding is L2-normalized, $s$ is defined as a dot-product function which represents the cosine similarity. Two triplets can be denoted as $L_{tri\_topic}$

and $L_{tri\_time}$, so the eventual loss ($L_{total}$) to be minimized has become $L_{total} = L_{tri\_topic} + L_{tri\_time}$. Through grid search, we could find that 0.1 and 0.1 are optimized values for $\tau_{topic}$ and $\tau_{time}$, respectively. Finally, we perform spherical k-means clustering to identify topic clusters. The Silhouette value is measured to determine the number of clusters.

## 3 Results

### 3.1 Embedding Results

Figure 1 illustrates two embedding examples from the various combinations on choosing $\tau$ in the case of South Korea. The figures are plotted via t-SNE by reducing dimensionality by 2. We could confirm that our hyperparameter setting (i.e., $\tau_{topic} = 0.1$, $\tau_{time} = 0.1$) results more distinctive clusters than other conditions. The same values for two $\tau$ may mean that the topic and time information equally contributes to the embeddings.

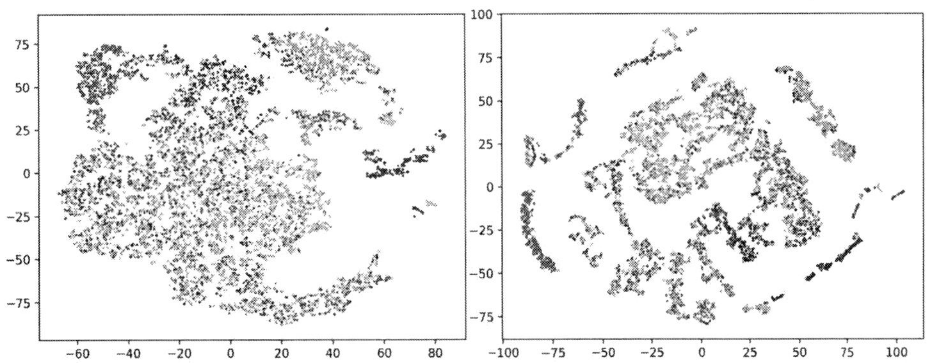

Figure 1: Embedding comparison via t-SNE between two different $\tau$ settings in the case of South Korea. $\tau_{topic} = 0.1$, $\tau_{time} = 0.01$ (left) whereas 0.1, 0.1 (our case, right).

### 3.2 Clustering Results with Evaluation

We then compare the clustering results within the South Korean case based on ablation studies, which are utilizing 1) LDA; 2) LDA+mBERT (concatenating two normalized outputs, then run k-means clustering); 3) LDA+mBERT+CL (our model). The statistics of the clustering results are presented in Table 1). The number of tweets per event of our model varies less than those of LDA, although our model has fewer events. We used the average standard deviation (SD) and standard error (SE) in timestamp as a metric to evaluate whether detected events share the same temporal information. Concerning the timestamp metric, our model shows the smallest time dissimilarity per event on average, meaning our model well reflects the temporal information in practice. By combining these two observations, we conclude our model smoothed LDA by successfully contemplating the time information together as planned.

| Metric | Statistics | LDA | LDA+mBERT | **LDA+mBERT+CL (ours)** |
|---|---|---|---|---|
| # of Events | Count | 50 (fixed) | 64 | 20 |
| # of Tweets | Mean (SD) | 182.38 (489.43) | 142.48 (136.63) | 455.95 (307.46) |
| Timestamp | Average SD | 0.25 | 0.24 | **0.16** |
| | Average SE | 0.03 | 0.02 | **0.01** |

Table 1: Statistics of the clustering results from three models in the case of South Korea.

### 3.3 Detected Events across Time by Country

For Iran and Vietnam, Figure 2 shows the trends of the detected events, respectively. When determining those countries' events, we have used the same hyperparameter values from the South Korean case. Particularly with South Korea, we have further qualitatively interpreted the events and merged similar topics, as depicted in Figure 3. For instance, total 20 topics detected from the South Korea data are labeled and merged into 13 discriminative topics. Tweet volumes became larger from mid-February as the number of confirmed cases abruptly rose due to a regional church outbreak, and it lasted until the end of March. During this period, the number of events was relatively small as people focused on a few events like news about the global confirmed cases. As the situation eased from April, the events became more diverse. Also, we could see that the rumor events were relatively steady across the whole period.

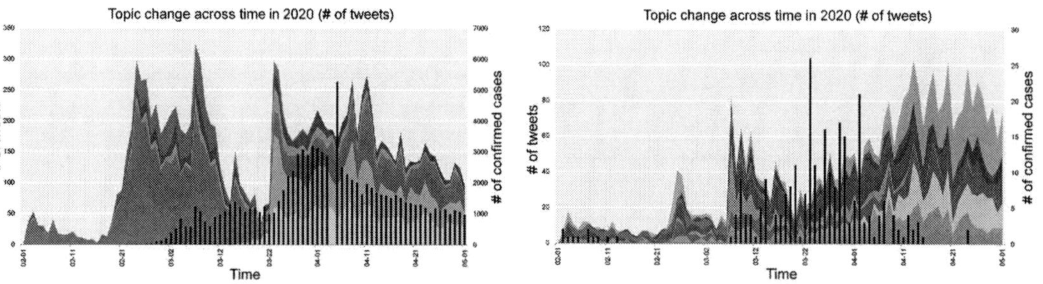


Figure 2: Daily event trends in Iran (left) and Vietnam (right). Black bar graphs represent the number of daily confirmed cases.

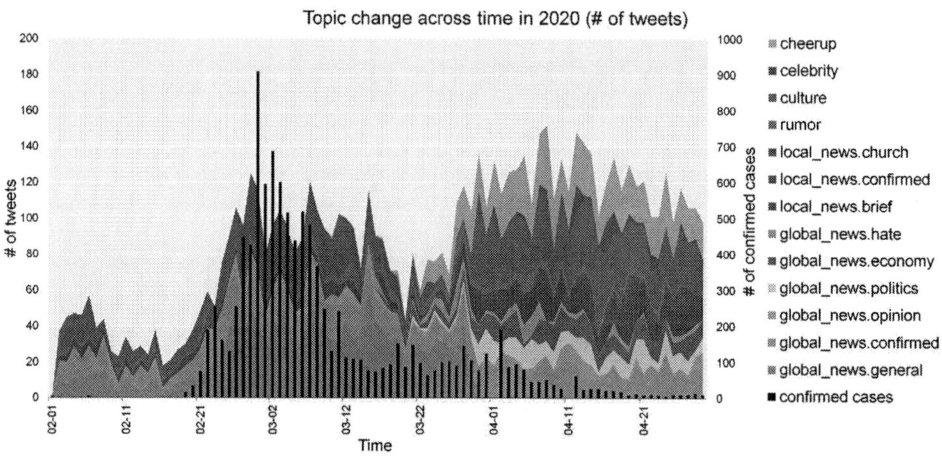


Figure 3: Daily event trends after qualitatively assessed in South Korea.

## 4 Discussion

We have extracted event trends based on the contextualized event detection model with CL in the paper. By introducing two kinds of the triplets: LDA-dependent and time-dependent triplets, our model efficiently trains the embedding to gather similar events within a short period. We also present the qualitative interpretation of the trends in South Korea as a possible application. As the proposed method can be executed by country, if we detect misinformation or disinformation prevalent in only one country first, we can quickly alarm other countries to deal with this issue preemptively.

For future studies, we can think of utilizing other topic modeling algorithms beyond LDA, like BTM (Yan et al., 2013) or DocNADE (Larochelle and Lauly, 2012) by considering temporal traits together, then compare the performance to the current model. Some research has shown the efficacy of variational autoencoder on modeling topics (Miao et al., 2016) in terms of both topic coherence and perplexity. Besides, the framework of the current work is retrospective, and we can also try to build a monitoring/analyzing framework for detecting events in real-time. By investigating how the risk communication on COVID-19 proceeds in real-time, it would be easier to react to misinformation immediately.

## Acknowledgements

This work was supported by the Institute for Basic Science (IBS-R029-C2).

## References

Farzindar Atefeh and Wael Khreich. 2015. A survey of techniques for event detection in twitter. *Computational Intelligence*, 31(1):132–164.

Elisabeth Beaunoyer, Sophie Dupéré, and Matthieu J Guitton. 2020. Covid-19 and digital inequalities: Reciprocal impacts and mitigation strategies. *Computers in Human Behavior*, page 106424.

David M Blei and John D Lafferty. 2006. Dynamic topic models. In *Proceedings of the 23rd international conference on Machine learning*, pages 113–120.

Bo Dai and Dahua Lin. 2017. Contrastive learning for image captioning. In *Advances in Neural Information Processing Systems*, pages 898–907.

Oguzhan Gencoglu. 2020. Large-scale, language-agnostic discourse classification of tweets during covid-19. *arXiv preprint arXiv:2008.00461*.

Hugo Larochelle and Stanislas Lauly. 2012. A neural autoregressive topic model. In *Advances in Neural Information Processing Systems*, pages 2708–2716.

David MJ Lazer, Matthew A Baum, Yochai Benkler, Adam J Berinsky, Kelly M Greenhill, Filippo Menczer, Miriam J Metzger, Brendan Nyhan, Gordon Pennycook, David Rothschild, et al. 2018. The science of fake news. *Science*, 359(6380):1094–1096.

Yishu Miao, Lei Yu, and Phil Blunsom. 2016. Neural variational inference for text processing. In *International conference on machine learning*, pages 1727–1736.

Martin Müller, Marcel Salathé, and Per E Kummervold. 2020. Covid-twitter-bert: A natural language processing model to analyse covid-19 content on twitter. *arXiv preprint arXiv:2005.07503*.

Sungkyu Park, Sungwon Han, Jeongwook Kim, Mir Majid Molaie, Hoang Dieu Vu, Karandeep Singh, Jiyoung Han, Wonjae Lee, and Meeyoung Cha. 2020. Risk communication in asian countries: Covid-19 discourse on twitter. *arXiv preprint arXiv:2006.12218*.

Umair Qazi, Muhammad Imran, and Ferda Ofli. 2020. Geocov19: A dataset of hundreds of millions of multilingual covid-19 tweets with location information.

Margaret E Roberts, Brandon M Stewart, Dustin Tingley, Edoardo M Airoldi, et al. 2013. The structural topic model and applied social science. In *Advances in neural information processing systems workshop on topic models: computation, application, and evaluation*, volume 4. Harrahs and Harveys, Lake Tahoe.

Xiaohui Yan, Jiafeng Guo, Yanyan Lan, and Xueqi Cheng. 2013. A biterm topic model for short texts. In *Proceedings of the 22nd international conference on World Wide Web*, pages 1445–1456.

**Association for Computational Linguistics**
209 N. Eighth Street
Stroudsburg, Pennsylvania 18360

ISBN 978-1-7138-2835-8